Whitetail Deer

NorthWord
Minnetonka, Minnesota

DEDICATION
For Paul, who fills my world with love and wonder.

© NorthWord Press, 2000

Photography © 2000: Bill Lea: front cover, pp. 8, 12-13, 22-23, 25, 26, 30, 38-39, 40; John R. Ford: pp. 4, 34-35; Mark Wallner/Wing It Wildlife: p. 5; Mark Raycroft: pp. 6-7, 9, 10, 20; Lisa & Mike Husar/Team Husar: p. 19; Donald M. Jones: p. 28; Robert McCaw: p. 36; Erwin & Peggy Bauer: p. 43; Michael H. Francis: back cover, pp. 15, 16, 44-45

Illustrations by John F. McGee
Designed by Russell S. Kuepper
Edited by Barbara K. Harold

NorthWord
11571 K-Tel Drive
Minnetonka, MN 55343
www.tnkidsbooks.com

Library of Congress Cataloging-in-Publication Data

Evert, Laura.
       Whitetail deer / text by Laura Evert ; illustrations by John F. McGee.
            p.   cm. — (Our wild world series)
       ISBN 1-55971-743-2 (softcover)
       1. White-tailed deer—Juvenile literature. I. McGee, John F. II. Title. III. Series.
       QL737.U55 E93 2000
       599.65'2--dc21   00-028351

Printed in Malaysia

CPSIA Tracking Information:
Selangor Darul Ehsan Malaysia
Date of Production: January 2010
Cohort: Batch # 1

Whitetail Deer

Laura Evert
Illustrations by John F. McGee

NORTHWORD
Minnetonka, Minnesota

THERE ARE AT LEAST 25 million whitetail deer in North America. And if you see one, you know how it got its name!

They can be found in all of the United States except Alaska and Hawaii. They are also found in six Canadian provinces, Mexico, Central America, and even as far south as Peru in South America.

Deer live almost everywhere in almost any habitat. A habitat is a specific place in the environment where animals (and people) can live. Swamps, meadows, prairies, woodlands, forests, and even cities and farmlands are all habitats where deer can be found. The best habitats for whitetails are the ones that provide them with three things: good cover, food, and water.

The large size of these antlers help tell that this is an older deer.

It is not unusual for mature, healthy whitetails to have twin babies.

Each deer spends almost all of its life in one specific area. This area is called its home range. A female's home range is about 1 square mile (2.6 square kilometers) in size. It also must have a good place to have babies and keep them hidden from predators. Males usually have bigger home ranges.

The edges of forests and woodlands are the best places for deer to live. There are plenty of trees and bushes for cover and there is usually a good water source nearby.

Streams, rivers, ponds, swamps, and lakes are all good water sources. Some deer, though, don't need to drink much water because they get enough in the food they eat.

Whitetail Deer
FUNFACT:

Biologists often use
the deer's scientific name,
Odocoileus virginianus.

In addition to drinking the water, whitetails walk
and swim in lakes and ponds to escape biting insects.

The plants and trees that are found in these areas provide the best food for deer. Deer are herbivores (HERB-uh-vorz), or plant-eating animals. They like to eat thick grasses, mosses, clover, juicy leaves, nuts, and especially fruit and berries like apples, blackberries, raspberries, and blueberries. They also eat the leaves of dogwood, aspen, and oak trees. These foods give the deer both nutrition and moisture.

The type of food that whitetail deer eat depends on the region where they live. In the southeastern United States deer are fond of grapes in the summer. In the Desert Southwest, deer often eat the fruit of the prickly pear cactus. And in areas near farmlands, deer feast on corn that has

Deer do not usually eat whole plants, but only the most nutritious and tender parts such as buds, leaves, and young stems.

fallen on the ground after harvesting. They also graze on the lush grasses of the surrounding pastures.

Deer that live in urban areas (places near or in cities) sometimes make people unhappy by eating the flowers, buds, and vegetables in gardens. Flowers that deer seem to prefer are roses and violets. Carrots, potatoes, and corn are among their favorite vegetables.

When eating, deer chew their food only enough to swallow it. When they find a safe place to rest they bring the food back up for grinding.

A deer does not have incisors, or middle teeth, on its upper jaw like most other animals and people have. But it does have them on the bottom jaw. It also has back teeth, called molars, on its upper and lower jaws, for grinding the food.

A deer grasps the food with its bottom incisors and uses its tongue to push the food against the roof of its mouth while pulling it inside for a quick chew.

Eating this way causes the branches and stems of plants to look ragged, so this is a good way to tell if a deer has been eating in the garden!

Whitetail Deer
FUNFACT:

An adult deer may eat 10 pounds (over 4 kilograms) of food per day.

Deer may rise up on their hind legs to reach their favorite fruit, nuts, and berries that are high off the ground.

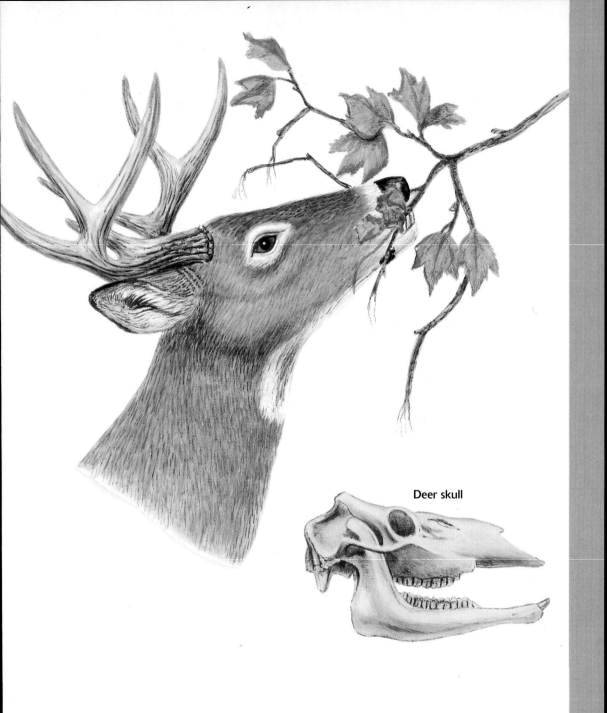

Deer skull

Pages 12-13: If there is plenty of food in the area,
groups of deer may graze together in the same field.

11

In winter, whitetails get less moisture from the food they eat, and if the streams and lakes are frozen over, they must eat snow for their water. At this time of year, there is less food, and deer have to look harder for it.

During the colder months in the snowy northern states, deer must dig with their hooves to uncover any remaining acorns or leftover vegetables. If the snow is too deep, they may have to eat the twigs and young branches of small bushes and the bark of cedar trees. These woody foods, called browse (BROWZ), are not very nutritious.

Just like a cow, a deer has four chambers in its stomach, which helps the deer eat this great variety of food. Since deer are timid and don't like to stay in one place for very long, they eat as much food as they can before finding a safe place to digest it.

When they have found a good place to rest after eating, they bring the quickly swallowed food back up and finish chewing it. This partly digested food is called cud, and is why deer and cows are called cud chewers. After the deer swallow their cud for the last time, it moves into a different chamber of the stomach to finish digesting.

Whitetail Deer
FUNFACT:

Each day, whitetails rest and sleep in a different "bed," which looks like an oval depression in the snow or leaves.

Even in the snow, deer rely on their well-used trails through the forest.
The trails lead to food and can be used as escape routes.

Deer do not have to turn their heads toward a sound to hear it better, they simply turn one or both of their ears.

The size of a deer depends on where it lives. Deer that live farther north are larger than deer that live in southern areas. This is because it takes more body heat to get through the cold winters of the North, so larger deer are more likely to survive. In the South, where temperatures are hotter, their bodies need to keep in less heat, so smaller bodies are better.

Adult male deer, called bucks, weigh about 175 pounds (79 kilograms) in the northern states and are about 6 feet long (183 centimeters) from nose to tail. Female deer, called does (DOZE), weigh about 122 pounds (55 kilograms) and are just over 4 feet (122 centimeters) long. Bucks stand about 3½ feet (107 centimeters) tall at the shoulder. Does are about 3 feet (91 centimeters) tall.

Southern deer are not usually as big. Those that live in Florida may only grow to weigh 80 pounds (36 kilograms). That's less than half the size of northern deer!

Northern whitetail deer have dark, gray-brown coats of hair in winter. Darker colors hold in the heat better. But by summertime, the northern deer have shed that coat and grown a lighter, reddish-brown one that southern deer have almost all year-round. The underside of a deer's neck and its belly are white. The underside of a deer's tail is also white.

A deer's coat is different in winter and summer by more than just the color. To prepare for winter, the deer grows a thick coat made of hairs that are hollow. It may seem hard to believe, but this helps the deer stay warm. The space inside each of the hairs is filled with air heated by the deer's body. The hair works the same way as insulation in a house does: It keeps the warm air in and the cold, wet air out.

The deer's summer coat is thinner and made of short, lightweight, solid hairs. The reddish brown color of the summer coat reflects the sunshine and keeps the deer from overheating on long, hot days. Deer go through life wearing just the right coat at the right time—warm in winter and cool in summer.

Since they are born in late spring, just when the heat of summer is starting, the color of a baby deer's coat is red-brown. Baby deer are called fawns. Scattered all over the fawn's coat are little white spots. The white spots help the fawn hide from danger. It is hard to see a fawn when it is lying on the ground because it blends in with its surroundings. This is called camouflage (KAM-uh-flaj).

Whitetail Deer
FUNFACT:

The spots on a fawn's coat usually disappear when it is about 3 months old.

The white spots on a fawn's coat help it hide among
the plants, leaves, and flowers of its habitat.

Scientists can identify deer by their antlers. Every set looks different—like human fingerprints do.

When you picture a whitetail deer in your mind, that deer probably has antlers on its head. Only bucks have antlers, which can be used to defend against predators. Wolves, coyotes, and cougars are all predators of deer. These animals hunt deer for food. Bears are also predators, and are especially dangerous to newborn fawns.

Pages 22-23: As the daylight hours begin to shorten in autumn, bucks begin to compete for does with shoving matches.

Unlike the horns on a cow, a buck's antlers are not hollow. Deer antlers are made of bone.

A buck's antlers may help him attract does. In the fall, bucks and does are ready to mate.

During this time, called the rut, bucks may use their antlers in contests with each other. They put their heads down and lock antlers while pushing back and forth. It is a contest of strength.

The buck that wins the contest is usually the strongest and healthiest. During these shoving matches, the bucks usually do not hurt each other.

The buck scrapes the ground with his hooves and leaves his scent, or odor, to attract a female. When a doe wants to mate with the buck, she finds his scrape and leaves her scent too. The buck uses her scent to help look for her. A buck may mate with up to 20 does per season.

A buck grows and sheds new antlers every year. And as the buck grows bigger each year, so do his antlers. A buck's antlers are usually the biggest they will ever be when he is 5 years old.

Bucks start to grow antlers in the spring, beginning in May or June. As the antlers grow, they are covered with a soft material called velvet. The velvet is made of nerves and blood vessels that supply nutrients to the growing antlers. The velvet dries out and falls off the hard antlers in the autumn, before the deer begin to mate. Bucks sometimes use branches to help them remove the velvet.

In the middle of winter, usually in January through March, bucks shed their antlers. Changes within the buck's body cause them to fall off. This does not hurt the buck, and in just a couple months he will start to grow a new set of antlers.

While a deer's antlers are covered with velvet, they may grow as much as one-half inch per day.

To help identify scents better, a deer wets its nose with its tongue before smelling.
This helps the odor stick to the nose longer.

Besides antlers, there are other parts of a whitetail's body that make it very different from other animals. Deer have very large noses, ears, and eyes. They help the deer in many ways. Most importantly, they help the deer detect and escape predators. They also help deer communicate with each other.

The deer's sense of smell is probably its most important feature. A deer can tell if another animal is nearby and even what kind of animal it is just from its scent. Deer can also tell how old the scent is. This means that if the scent is old, the deer knows that the danger is past. But if the scent is new, the deer runs away as quickly as its legs can carry it.

Deer also use their sense of smell to find and identify each other. Each deer has its own scent, and as it walks along and stops to eat, it leaves some scent behind. Scent is left in a deer's tracks, and on branches and plants that it brushes against. It also leaves scent in its droppings, which is called scat. A deer's scat looks like small clusters of grapes, but the hard little clusters are more oval-shaped than round. And depending on what the deer ate, the scat may be different colors.

Whitetail Deer
FUNFACT:

Deer usually live 4 to 5½ years, but they may live as long as 12 years.

Scent is what a mother deer uses to find her way back to her fawns after she has left them to feed. Newborn fawns do not have scent, but she can retrace her steps by following her own scent. And a young deer finds its mother in a group of deer by memorizing her scent.

Whitetail deer also use their noses to find food. Other than sniffing for scent of the actual food, deer also try to find the scent of a trail left by other deer. If they smell a trail that other deer have used a lot, they follow it hoping to find food at the end of it.

Fawns imprint on their mother soon after birth, which means that they learn to recognize her by her smell and her sounds.

A deer's hearing is very important to its survival. Deer have large ears that are cup shaped. These big ears work almost like satellite dishes, scooping up and collecting all the sounds and transmitting them to their brains. Deer can move their ears to point in almost any direction, and each ear can move in a different direction separately from the other.

Triangulation (try-an-gu-LAY-shun) is how deer can easily figure out where a sound is coming from and how far away it is. Triangulation works this way: The deer first points both ears toward the sound. It then figures out how long it took the sound to reach one ear and then the other. The deer can then pinpoint the exact location and distance the sound came from—all in a split second!

A deer's small hooves help it run faster because there is less contact with the ground to slow it down. The hooves are also sharp, which helps the deer get good traction.

A deer's sense of sight is not as good as its hearing, but it is still remarkable. Deer have much better sight than people have when the light is low, like at dawn and dusk. That is why deer are crepuscular (krip-US-kyoo-ler), or most active in the early morning and late evening. Deer constantly search for food, and since they have to watch out for predators while they eat, it makes sense that they move about when they have an advantage over their enemies.

Whitetails can see very well in bright light. And they have a much wider field of view than people have—in fact, their view is 50 percent wider than a human's. But deer do not see colors very well, especially reds and oranges.

Deer have legs that are stronger and faster than they appear. A deer's legs are long and thin so that it can move quickly through the woods. Underbrush such as fallen logs and small shrubs are not obstacles for deer—they simply step or jump over them. When running from predators, deer use quick bursts of speed to escape. They also run in a zigzag pattern, jumping over trees and bushes again and again, hoping to slow down the shorter-legged enemy chasing them.

At the end of their graceful legs deer have narrow, sharp hooves. Each hoof is actually made up of two toes. A little farther up the back of the deer's leg are two more toes, called dew claws.

Whitetail Deer
FUNFACT:

Whitetails are related to moose, elk, caribou, and mule deer.

Deer are called perfect walkers. This means that when they walk, their back feet touch down exactly where their front feet had been. This works well for the secretive deer since they like to walk without making a noise. They know that if they manage to set their front foot down silently, the back foot will not make a sound either.

Whitetail tracks look like upside-down commas facing each other, almost like a heart shape. They are especially easy to see if they are in soft sand, mud, or snow.

A deer's tail is probably its most unique feature. Deer rely on their tails for communication with each other. A deer's tail is commonly called its flag.

Deer can tell what other deer are thinking just by looking at the position of their tails. When a deer is alarmed, it raises its tail high. Other deer that can see the white of the tail know to be ready to run away from possible danger. If it turns out to be a false alarm, the deer will swish its tail from side to side once, as if saying, "Everything's okay. No need to worry."

Whitetail Deer
FUNFACT:

Deer are strong swimmers, and sometimes use a river or lake as an escape from predators.

A doe also raises her tail when she is ready to mate. She holds it sideways to signal a buck. When a buck sees a doe with her tail held sideways, he knows that he probably will not be chased away.

Fawns learn at a young age to use their tails to communicate like the adults do. But they also wag their tails, just like a puppy does when it is happy and playful.

When the tail is lowered against the body, it usually means that no danger is present and that the deer is calm. When the tail is down, you can barely see the outline of white around it.

Sometimes deer lower their tails when fleeing, or running away, from an enemy. This way the predator does not have an easy-to-see target bobbing through the woods.

As fawns grow older and stronger, their camouflaging spots fade and their mother teaches them to be alert for danger.

Sometimes during the rut, a buck's antlers may be damaged.
The tips or points may be broken off.

Adult deer have several ways of defending themselves against enemies. They can kick with their powerful legs and sharp hooves, and bucks can use their antlers to chase off attackers. But the deer's best defense is to run away as quickly as possible. Deer have been observed running at over 40 miles (65 kilometers) per hour! Their long legs make it easy to jump over obstacles that stop other animals in their tracks—even fences.

Deer can jump over a 7-foot-high (2.1 meters) fence from a standing start. While running they can leap over an 8-foot-high (2.4 meters) fence. This makes them very hard to catch, and predators usually don't even try to catch them if there's room for the deer to run.

Mother whitetails protect their babies from predators as well as they can. When a fawn is first born, the doe carefully licks the fawn clean so it has no scent and is less likely to be found by other animals while the mother is away looking for food. She leaves the fawn in a safe hiding place, usually in a thicket of sticks or bed of leaves. Although a fawn can run, its best defense is to lie very still until the danger passes.

Whitetail Deer
FUNFACT:

The largest whitetail ever recorded lived in Minnesota and weighed 511 pounds.

If a fence is in the way, a deer may
just jump over it to feed on the other side.

If a predator finds the fawn, the mother will fiercely defend it. She may put her head down and ram the other animal, or kick it as hard as she can. But her best strategy is to raise her white tail and run away from the fawn. She hopes that the predator will see her tail as a target and run after her and away from the fawn.

When she has run a safe distance and is sure the predator is not following her, she circles back and moves her fawn to a new hiding place.

Whitetail Deer
FUNFACT:

A 1-year-old buck is called a yearling, and usually grows thin spikes or forked antlers.

Newborn fawns are weak and wobbly, but they grow quickly and are soon able to walk and run.

Deer do not often call out to each other, but they do make several sounds, or vocalizations (vo-kul-ize-A-shuns), when they need to communicate.

When a deer is startled or frightened, it snorts. A snort is a quick, loud burst of air through the nose that sounds a little like a blast through a horn.

If the deer senses danger, but knows that it is not very close by, it snorts several times in a row to alert other deer. When the others hear the snort they know they have to be ready to flee. Both bucks and does snort.

Adult whitetail deer also grunt. If a doe feels that her food is being taken, for example, she lets the other deer know it by grunting. The other deer will usually move away in order to avoid a fight. A buck's grunt gets louder and longer if he feels he is being challenged.

Deer also have softer grunts and calls that they use when mating or locating one another. They do not make sounds unless they have to, however, because they do not want predators to hear them.

Fawns make the most noises. They use a soft, gentle whine when they are nursing. When a fawn can't locate its mother, it bleats, like a lamb. Usually the doe comes back to the fawn when she hears it bleat. But if she is eating and does not sense danger, she may not return right away. The bleats get louder and sound more like a cry until she returns.

When a fawn is in real danger it bawls loudly. This noise brings the doe back immediately, ready to defend her young.

Deer don't usually live together in one big group. Most does form small groups that stay close to one another. A doe group is usually led by the oldest female, or matriarch (MAY-tree-ark). Other deer in the group may be her sisters, nieces, daughters, and even granddaughters. Very young males are also allowed in this group.

The matriarch is the one who decides where the group will go to find food. The other does show her respect and allow her and her offspring to eat first. If another doe does not respect the lead doe, she might be punished with a nudge or kick.

Bucks do not usually live or travel together. They prefer to be alone, except for mating time when they are with the does.

Sometimes, when there is enough food for everyone, young males band together in bachelor (BACH-uh-ler) groups. The group usually breaks up when the rut begins and they compete with each other for the right to mate with a doe. The strongest bucks with the largest antlers usually win the battles.

After mating in the fall, does must wait until May or June for their fawns to be born. When a doe is ready to give birth she goes off alone to the place she has selected to have her baby, called the nursery area. She will chase other deer away that try to follow her. Young does usually have only one baby. Older does may have twins or even triplets.

Fawns usually weigh about 5 pounds (2.25 kilograms) when born. Within 20 minutes they are able to stand and walk! Then the mother doe leads it away from the nursery area to hide.

If a mother has more than one fawn she takes each of them to a different hiding place. This way, if a predator happens to find one of the babies, the other should be safe. And it is easier for a mother to protect her fawns one at a time.

This group of does can eat more safely,
since there are many eyes and ears on the alert for danger.

Deer living in southern areas have bigger ears.
This helps them lose extra body heat in order to stay cooler.

A fawn doubles its weight within its first 2 weeks. It drinks its mother's milk until it is about 3 months old, then it learns which foods are good to eat and where to find them. During this time, the doe usually keeps her fawns away from the other deer in her group. As autumn nears, she and her fawns rejoin the group and they graze for food together. They need to eat as much as possible to put on weight for the coming winter.

Whitetails do not hibernate in the winter like some other animals do. They spend their time searching for food and staying warm under their winter coats. Starvation in winter is the biggest threat to the deer's survival, especially in the northern states where there is deep snow and cold temperatures. During this time they move around as little as possible in order to conserve their energy.

In the spring, all the deer that survived the winter are not only older, they are wiser. They have learned how to hide from predators and where to find the best food. And they will teach these things to the new fawns as the year begins again.

Internet Sites

You can find out more interesting information about whitetail deer and lots of other wildlife by visiting these Internet sites.

www.animal.discovery.com   Discovery Channel Online

www.kidsplanet.org   Defenders of Wildlife

www.nationalgeographic.com/kids   National Geographic Society

www.nwf.org/kids   National Wildlife Federation

www.worldwildlife.org   World Wildlife Fund

http://nature.org   The Nature Conservancy

Index

Titles available in the Our Wild World Series:

ALLIGATORS AND CROCODILES
ISBN 978-1-55971-859-2

BATS
ISBN 978-1-55971-969-8

BISON
ISBN 978-1-55971-775-5

BLACK BEARS
ISBN 978-1-55971-742-7

BUTTERFLIES
ISBN 978-1-55971-967-4

CARIBOU
ISBN 978-1-55971-812-7

CHIMPANZEES
ISBN 978-1-55971-845-5

COUGARS
ISBN 978-1-55971-788-5

COYOTES
ISBN 978-1-55971-983-4

DOLPHINS
ISBN 978-1-55971-776-2

EAGLES
ISBN 978-1-55971-777-9

FALCONS
ISBN 978-1-55971-912-4

GORILLAS
ISBN 978-1-55971-843-1

HAWKS
ISBN 978-1-55971-886-8

LEOPARDS
ISBN 978-1-55971-796-0

LIONS
ISBN 978-1-55971-787-8

LIZARDS
ISBN 978-1-55971-857-8

MANATEES
ISBN 978-1-55971-778-6

MONKEYS
ISBN 978-1-55971-849-3

MOOSE
ISBN 978-1-55971-744-1

ORANGUTANS
ISBN 978-1-55971-847-9

OWLS
ISBN 978-1-55971-915-5

PENGUINS
ISBN 978-1-55971-810-3

POLAR BEARS
ISBN 978-1-55971-828-8

PRAIRIE DOGS
ISBN 978-1-55971-884-4

SEA TURTLES
ISBN 978-1-55971-746-5

SEALS
ISBN 978-1-55971-826-4

SHARKS
ISBN 978-1-55971-779-3

SNAKES
ISBN 978-1-55971-855-4

TIGERS
ISBN 978-1-55971-797-7

TURTLES
ISBN 978-1-55971-861-5

VULTURES
ISBN 978-1-55971-918-6

WHALES
ISBN 978-1-55971-780-9

WHITETAIL DEER
ISBN 978-1-55971-743-4

WILD HORSES
ISBN 978-1-55971-882-0

WOLVES
ISBN 1-55971-748-9

NorthWord
Minnetonka, Minnesota

New Glass

NewGlass

Otto B. Rigan   PHOTOGRAPHS BY CHARLES FRIZZELL

SAN FRANCISCO BOOK COMPANY, INC.   *San Francisco 1976*

FOR MY PARENTS

Library of Congress Cataloging in Publication Data

Rigan, Otto B. 1950-
    New glass

    1. Glass painting and staining.   2.   Glass paint-
ers.   I.   Frizzell, Charles, 1941- II.   Title.
NK5310.R53   748.5′913   76-22734
ISBN 0-913374-52-0

Simon and Schuster Order Number 22380

Trade distribution by Simon and Schuster
A Gulf + Western Company

10 9 8 7 6 5 4 3 2 1

Grateful acknowledgment is made to Susan Anderson for her valuable assistance in the early stages of the text.

Contents

*A sixty-four-page section of color
photographs follows page 22.*

Introduction

Stained glass strikes a responsive chord in each of us. No one knows exactly where or when stained glass was first used, but we all know we like it. The play of light through glass, transforming interiors with a shower of colors, has always been an aesthetic and emotional delight.

For most people a general impression of the stained-glass craft ranges from Chartres Cathedral to Tiffany lamps to decorative windows in Victorian houses. There is a new expression of this old medium, however, and it is not Gothic, Victorian, or Art Nouveau, nor is it hanging over your dining room table. The new glass, though having its roots in the traditional *craft*, has shattered the boundaries of convention and style to evolve into an independent *art*. The new glass shows the spirit of the individual artists in styles that reflect humankind's changing, eclectic consciousness. The only thing the new glass has in common with its predecessors is the medium itself.

The stained-glass craft has traditionally been impervious to radical change. Until this century there was no pressure for the glass field to revolutionize itself. The medieval windows of the twelfth to fourteenth centuries were a perfect complement to Gothic architecture. Like tapestries in color and design, their appeal was primarily as pattern, and personal iconography, if any, was decidedly secondary. Such windows were made by craftsmen and artisans working within narrow limits.

The coming of the Renaissance to Northern Europe slightly changed this architectural concept as Gothic windows slowly evolved into glass paintings through which light could filter. They were non-architectural in the sense that the buildings were to the windows no more than frames for the artists' "canvasses" executed in glass. But, though freed somewhat from its strong architectural dependence, the glass medium in the post-Renaissance period was far too costly for development by individuals in the secular world, and, as individual expression, glass art remained secondary to the art of studio painting. Glass art has had little identity as a personal medium up to present times, but has consistently reflected the interchange among art, architecture, and wealthy institutional patrons.

Another inhibitor of change in the evolution of the craft was its perceived purpose. Stained-glass windows from the Middle Ages to the present were mainly ecclesiastical or monumental statements. And usually only the Church could afford such extravagance. With the development and growing affluence of the middle class after the Industrial Revolution, glass occasionally turned up in the secular world, but mostly as decorative coats of arms or the standard diamond-shaped "Dutch windows." It was not until the late nineteenth century and the glass of Louis Comfort Tiffany and his peers and imitators that glass made any real penetration into secular life. Victorian and

Tiffany-styled windows could be found in homes, but they still had not broken the aesthetic links with the traditions of the craft. Victorian windows were merely decorative and Tiffany was attempting to emulate the concepts of the medievalists in a contemporary fashion.

Despite the realities of space travel, world wars, the effects of mass media, and the bomb, most glass artisans of this century have continued to work within the traditional standards of stained glass. Those standards, holdovers of an aesthetic mentality from previous centuries, have frequently been translated into bad reproductions of styles that are not relevant to our times.

Post-World War II Germans were the first to challenge tradition and to signal a transition from glass craft to glass art. The Germans had nothing to lose. They had lost a war and a great many of their churches and public buildings. They were not interested in rebuilding the past. New, emotionally clean, graphic windows were therapy for the subdued human spirit and ideal for the simple, modern parish churches and public buildings that were being built to replace the old. German artists purified the glass field by incorporating unpainted glass in their designs, thereby returning to the natural integrity of their materials, lead and glass. But even this contemporary German art has developed within the shadow of architectural limitation.

In the late 1970s, especially on the West Coast of North America, suddenly there don't seem to be any limits. This may be a function of a place and a time where popular culture continuously breaks its limits and where popular architecture is a composite of all styles from brown-shingled funk houses and geodesic domes to 1970s "moderne" and the golden arches. More likely, the pioneering, limit-shattering art of the new glass is not a purely western phenomenon or movement at all but springs up at a time when the American middle class has more leisure, is better educated and more diversified in interests than ever before, and when the search for expansive ideals and life-styles is at an all-time high. In any case, the new glass shows a new spirit in an ancient medium: contemporary culture is increasingly eclectic and so are the varied styles of the new glass artists.

The new breed of glass artist presented in this book seems determined to explore the medium for all of its possibilities, to shape it into a true art that is as responsive to the individual as to the current world. The shift from craft to art is complete.

Most of us think of art as something that only happens in museums and galleries. It is exciting to witness an exuberant new art form that relates to homes, everyday public places, and unexpected environmental sites, and, of greater importance, connects directly with people. The new glass, as you will see, has the capacity to evoke a positive response from the community as a whole—art connoisseur and wheat farmer alike.

As a painter, I recognize in the new glass a vital alternative to the more confounding, cerebral world of contemporary art. There is plenty of good

Entrance hall window, Ubach-Palenberg Public Baths. Ludwig Schaffrath, 1974.

art being shown in galleries, but most people won't see it. Somehow the gallery experience is unessential in everyday life. The new glass artists are bridging the distance between the community and the formal art world.

This new glass surely deserves documentation, which is one purpose of this book, but the diversified group of artists represented here did not lend themselves to being gathered up and placed neatly beneath the banner of something so categorical and defined as an "art movement" or "school." Still, since the human mind always tries to organize, sort, and individuate, I groped toward a definition. When I stumbled upon the phrase "omni-movement" I was delighted. As "omni" implies "all things combined," so my tag "omni-movement" expresses an art movement that is without a declared manifesto, statement of purpose, or any restriction whatever.

Personal. Individual. Alive. Fresh. These simple adjectives apply to the new glass. Just as each artist included here is a growing, breathing statement of humanity, so is the art that reflects him or her. The subject matter and approaches are as diversified as the artists themselves, and as long as the artists continue to evolve and change in the dramatic ways shown in this book they will produce a glass art that is neither static nor stale.

There are two general directions for the new glass artists. One is the "commission" approach (the tie to the architectural tradition), the other the autonomous approach. The artist on commission designs windows to harmonize with the physical style and function of a structure and to reflect the lives of the people who live in or use the building. Such windows are "walls of glass." This art—as in the days of the artisans—is subservient to architecture, but the sites and patrons of today are infinitely varied. To design and build an autonomous stained-glass work is to create a window panel for no particular structural opening, space, or client. But to speak of such polar extremes is simplistic. Of twenty-four artists documented in these pages there are twenty-four distinctly different aesthetic orientations. Imagine a football field with its end-zone goals. One goal is the purest interpretation of the autonomous philosophy, the other of the architectural philosophy. On the 50-yard line we release twenty-four jack rabbits. . . .

Many of these artists feel skittish about their work. On the one hand they are the budding roses, the creative thinkers, the revolutionaries in a field dominated by traditionalists and hobbyists, on the other they must make a living. Clients (commissions) often want what they are sure of (history, tradition) and are afraid of what an artist may produce. It is still an expensive medium, and it can be frustrating for the artist with little money and too few "right" commissions.

Who is creating the new glass? Some are formally trained artists, painters and sculptors among them, who have served apprenticeships in the medium. But most are from unexpected backgrounds—a railroad switchman, a body-and-fender man, graduates in English literature, physics, and philosophy. All have found in glass a means to express their unique individuality. They are all seers and trend-setters who are putting social and visual conventions into new perspectives.

Because of their diversity of personal approaches to glass art, I chose to let each artist speak directly to the reader in his or her own words. As with any visual art the visual object is the artist's primary statement, but this sharing of stories, philosophies, and goals behind each artist's particular works seemed too exciting to miss and a valuable means of insight into the human beings who create the art. Each artist was encouraged to say whatever he or she felt would be most representative. Some of their communications to me were fluid and personal; others, structured and formal. Many statements were received as lengthy essays, others as scribbled notes. Some of the statements are philosophical; others are analytic discussions of the techniques of particular windows. I hope this book will be as interesting to you for what it says by and about the people who make the art as it is for what it shows of the new glass art.

Otto B. Rigan

Atwater, California
June 1976

New Glass

Jad King

Jad, as part of his daily routine, drives his ochre-colored 1949 Plymouth from his comfortable, secluded cabin in the Lafayette foothills to his studio in Berkeley, California. It wasn't easy for me to find the studio. He works in a small, enclosed loft space in the rear part of a Chinese restaurant, and to reach it I had to walk down a narrow alley calling out his name. Once I found him, it was easy to feel comfortable with Jad. He talks softly, and while he works, plays such environmental sounds as Gregorian chants or Peruvian flute music.

Jad had been a medical illustrator, a television technician, and a graphic artist before arriving at the medium of glass. His glass work is organic in that it seems to be continuously changing, growing. His diversity of approach to the medium attracts unusual and different commissions, which run the gamut from geodesic domes to mansions to condominiums.

Most of Jad's windows are constructed in the copper-foil method, a

Untitled Victorian panel. Reworked 1975. 26½ × 43 inches.
Jad was commissioned to repaint what he considered an already overpainted antique window panel. Given the approval of the client, Jad superimposed the arm and cloth into the design, creating this surreal statement of his disapproval of the excessive use of paint on glass.

Jad King in his studio preparing a panel for soldering. The finished panel will be installed in a free-form sculpted door marking the entryway to a private wine cellar.

3

Tree Mandala. 1973. 6-foot diameter. The relative juxtaposition of a large oak tree and the window opening inspired the design in this residence in the Santa Cruz hills. Just as the geodesic dome shape is conceived through a mathematical formula, Jad designed in glass a branch of the oak tree, repeated the motif six times, and fitted it into the opening matrix.

Exterior view of *Tree Mandala* and domes.

technique usually reserved for Tiffany-like lamp construction. Copper foiling is the process of wrapping the outside edge of every piece of glass that is to be assembled into a window panel with a strip of ribbon-thin copper. All the edges are then bound together with a metallic solder. This process, unlike the traditional method of using a lead channel as the structural binder, allows for greater detail and more complex design, which is exactly what attracts Jad. The drawback of copper foiling, however, is that it is so time consuming. Considering that the stained-glass craft is one of the most complex arts ever created, Jad's use of the foil technique and the large sizes of many of his commissions must be weighed as heroic feats of patience.

I consider these years I've done stained glass as my apprenticeship to the medium. I have not worked in any one school or style. My approach has been to try to respond to each commission on an entirely individual basis. The windows should become a synthesis of their environment, my client's tastes and interests, and my continued exploration of the medium. Even my autonomous or independent windows explore many directions. Each is created to explore some technique I'd like to play with, like sand blasting, the third dimension, or the incorporation of the holographic image. . . .

I harbor a creative anger toward restrictions as to what is valid that both tradition and some of my glass peers place on glass.

Glass/light is magic to me, and anything that strengthens that interaction is a valid use of the medium to me. I doubt my apprenticeship to the medium will ever be over. . . .

4

Paul Marioni

Many glass artists who know Paul mention their respect for him as the explorer, the "technical virtuoso" of the new stained glass. I agree, for he pushes himself just as the inventors he enjoyed reading about as a child; exploring and developing technique and effects in a field stifled by traditional taboos. Driven to explore and measure the distance between illusion and reality, Paul seems to discover and invent techniques as a means of achieving illusionary ends. The result is an enriched palette for stained glass: Plexiglas tubes, Fresnel lenses, two-way mirrors, polarized glass, headlights, X-rays, photographic images, and whatever else may seem right.

How does a "technical virtuoso" in stained glass begin his career? As an English and philosophy graduate? That's how Paul did it, but he soon realized he couldn't *do* anything with his degree so he went into body-and-fender work. That work eventually proved too limiting and Paul found himself gravitating toward change. At that time he met Judy Raffael, who was already a glass artist, and they became friends. Judy is responsible for Paul's apprenticeship to the glass medium, which was anything but the standard approach. Traditionally, the stained-glass student spends three years in apprenticeship, most of that time performing the more undesirable chores that precede the actual event of designing and assembling a window. Paul's formal apprenticeship was five days of informal instruction from Judy. This introduction to stained glass marked the end of Paul's body-and-fender work and the beginning of an important contribution to the new directions the medium would take.

Paul's studio is in the attic of his brown-shingled house in Mill Valley, California. His working and living abound in eclectic acquisitiveness: hundreds of post cards, posters, and significant trivia pepper the walls. There are shells, rocks, plants, and even a pet rabbit that patrols the floors, pruning the houseplants and making it difficult to walk freely . . . altogether the place is a visual and sensuous extravaganza. There is a bust of Lincoln on the roof, a stained-glass window of "Mount Tamalpais blowing smoke rings" over the fireplace (the *real* Mount Tamalpais is just a few miles away), and a clear Plexiglas dining table and chairs. Both of Paul's cars are body-and-fender wrecks.

There is a certain impatient genius in Paul's character. He discovered the medium in impatience, and perhaps that same drive will lead him away from stained glass. He says that he would "drop it all to be able to play jazz on the tenor sax," and he is presently taking lessons to that end.

I often put 150 to 200 hours into a window but I'm more idea oriented, so that my head is three or four or ten windows ahead of my work and it's like carrying a weight behind me 'til I execute the idea.

5

Dali. 1971. 27½ × 26 inches. Collection of the artist.

This window is much more "active" than any photograph can document. Every piece of blue-gray glass used for the hair has a piece of Fresnel lens impressed onto the glass. (A Fresnel lens is a sheet of plastic fabricated in a way that creates a fish-eye effect when looked through.) The result is that the hair seems to be in constant motion, much like the snake serpents from the head of the mythological Medusa. The right eye is a piece of two-way mirror glass with a beveled edge on the mirrored side. The eye can be removed from the window and hung from a small attached chain. The left eye is made from a convex mirror, which gives an illusion of infinity when looked at closely as it keeps repeating into itself. The throat has a small doorway that actually functions. The doorknobs are small silver hands reaching in both directions.

Paul Marioni

Dali. Detail of throat section.

NERVE

    I was guest lecturing at a school in Washington, and staying with a teacher from the school who had a real nice house in the mountains behind Seattle. The whole front of the house is a wall of paned glass. The view is spectacular: elevation 2,500 feet overlooking rolling hills, the sound, the ocean, the islands—beautiful. I was really wanting to do some work and had no materials with me, so I got this idea to take a glass cutter and score and break each pane to outline the view. My host wasn't home at the time and I didn't even really know him, but he was considered Mr. Avant-Garde in glass so I figured he wouldn't mind if I busted his wall of glass. So, I made the first scratch in the first pane and the whole piece of glass went to hell. A friend was with me and he was stunned at seeing what I'd done and asked me if I knew what I was doing. I told him the idea had just struck me and he said I sure had a lot of nerve to screw up this wall. So I got a piece of clear glass, cut it the size of the pane I'd knocked out, wrote the word "nerve" in it, cut it, tapped it and replaced it. That's what got me started doing the cracked-glass series.

CADILLAC

    I was working as a body man when I did CADILLAC. . . . *I cut the lenses off a headlight. . . . The chrome is a two-way mirror that you can see through during the day and that comes alive at night. That's exciting.*

DALI

    I had started seeing that you could use anything you wanted to get any effect you wanted. Whenever I'd get a few bucks, I'd send away to Edmunds Scientific Catalogue for optical tricks. So I ended up with this bag of tricks and decided to use them all in one window. I didn't know much about Salvador Dali's work at the time, but I'd seen him on the news doing things like walking an anteater through the Paris subways and decided to use him for subject matter because he had such a colorful personality. I wanted a flamboyant subject to use all these tricks in. . . . I worked for six

Cadillac. 1971. Day detail. Berkeley, California, residence.

Cadillac. Night detail.

Nerve. 1974. Collection of the artist.

The Tin Man Buried by Words. 1975. Constructed with the assistance of Fritz Dreisbach.

The Tin Man Buried by Words. Detail of hand.

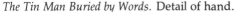

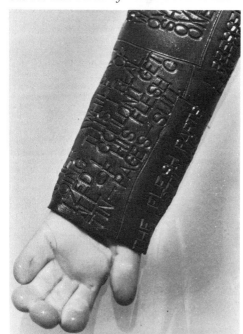

months designing this window so that none of the optical tricks would be too over-powering. It usually takes me a month or so to draw a window. I have a hard time getting the perspective.

THE TIN MAN BURIED BY WORDS

About every two years I have a horrifying dream that I don't wake up from to escape. I remain asleep and face whatever terror my subconscious offers me. When I've confronted that terror, I'll go on to another, then another, and sometimes another more horrible dream, face it, go through it, so by the time I'm done, I've faced all the things I'd been afraid to face for a long time. When I wake up I feel an enormous boost in my self-confidence that I was able to deal with whatever was buried in my subconscious. I've learned through this to trust my dream state, and as a result I've learned to trust myself more in waking life. Because I trust my dreams I get a lot of material from them. Like the TIN MAN—that's directly, 100 per cent from a dream. I realized that there'd be someone who'd think it was weird or grotesque or ugly, but I resisted changing it because that's the way it looked in my dream. In my dream it was a friend of mine wearing a tin suit that was made up of pages from a book, overlapping like shingles. He was embar-rassed about something and I was trying to cover him with his suit. He was soft, like Jello, really fleshy. I'd push him into one side of his suit and he'd sort of ooze out the other. I'd push in his head and his foot would fly out and it was like he couldn't be con-tained, so I ended up lying on top of him, covering the parts that wouldn't tuck in with my own body. I think that maybe it was myself I was trying to hide.

7

Kerry Kelly

John Bentley

Kerry Kelly and a stained-glass environment he created for a Victoria, British Columbia, residence.

Kerry started his professional life as a chemical engineer in Sarnia, Ontario. He quickly became disillusioned with corporate hypocrisies, the routine of it all, and the state of the artwork he was seeing in the galleries. ("A classic situation. I knew I could do better myself.") In the early 1970s he moved back to his native Victoria, British Columbia, to set up a studio. He began by producing ink-line and wash work, then a series of meticulous pencil drawings. Kerry's involvement with stained glass began before the recent craze for the craft had produced a retail market for hobby kits and how-to-do-it books. He had to teach himself the technique and scout out the materials on his own. In his search for information and supply sources, Kerry met and began to communicate with other glass artists, mainly those in California.

Kerry's explorations into the medium have produced a series of windows that vary greatly in purpose and feel. He has worked in both an architectural and a personal, autonomous form. Most of his work has an abstracted, organic feel, often plant-like, sometimes flesh-like. His color ranges from very soft, muted tones to windows with an unusually rich palette. Many of Kerry's autonomous panels are produced in miniature scale, with subject matter ranging from surrealistic cloud forms to a visual commentary on his own sexuality. In all his works it is apparent that Kerry is investigating his inner self as well as the physical qualities of the medium.

I was visiting a small glass company that was going out of business, and they had a batch of beautiful old stained glass that had been sitting there for years. I bought it all. I knew it was right for me. It combined so many things. I loved working line, and there it was in the lead work. I loved color but wasn't really attracted to painting, and there it was in the glass. I liked the idea of making art, of working with my hands, and there it was in the building of the windows. When I saw what some of the California artists were doing it blew me away. The range of styles and ideas that are possible in stained glass are just beginning to be explored.

I guess I don't really have a lot to say about my work or my relationship with it at this point. Still being a young man, I've relegated the responsibility of forming a philosophy to my old age when I hope I'll have a little better perspective on things.

Untitled. 21-inch diameter.
Collection of the artist.

P.M.B. 28 × 29 inches. Entryway to a Victoria, British Columbia, residence.

8

Fred Abrams

Fred apparently has a love-hate relationship with his city and the way it relates to him and his stained-glass panels. At one moment he speaks with anticipatory conviction of the time he will leave the Los Angeles basin and in the same breath expresses his marriage to the phenomenon of that city.

One thing is sure, his tongue-in-cheek humor as realized in his glass work is directly dependent on southern California style and culture. The subject matter of his windows expresses his total familiarity with the Los Angeles aesthetic. Fred's windows are not unique in structure or physical technique, but rather in choice of subject and purpose. They are a contradiction to the romanticized "beautiful window" concept that we have been conditioned by tradition to expect.

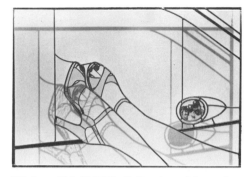

Who's on Third? 1975. Collection of the artist.

L.A., the town where people come to "make it." L.A., the media capital, where ads are made to sell us images of the "good life." L.A., where buildings are torn down as fast as they are built. L.A., a town full of illusions and unrealistic dreams. L.A., where beauty is in the eye of the ad man. L.A., where being on top is the name of the game. L.A., where if you're not on top, you're nowhere.

I worked for over a year in a small cottage in Santa Monica Canyon (probably the most exclusive, rustic environment in the city), with springs and creeks surrounding me. My place was one of the first to be built in the area, a "long twenty-five years ago." Slowly, trees were cut and large homes took their place. The owner died, and his wife sold the house. In desperation, all I could find was a studio with no windows and four white walls in an industrial area. My work became almost colorless. Albino-stained glass. I found myself fascinated with the internal structures of undersea creatures.

Feeding Polyp of Obelia (Internal Structure). 1974. Collection of the artist.

Like a mad scientist working in his basement, I experimented with glass. I tried to put the brain of a chicken in one window. I tried to find the cure for cancer. Some people thought I was creating a monster. But, as I saw it, I had realized that beauty was something that originated from within *and that the most beautiful window I could create would not stop smog.*

With WHO'S ON THIRD?*, I questioned one's perception of beauty. It took a subject that most anyone could relate to: a woman's legs and her stylish shoes. But the significance lies within what is not visible in the picture. The clear glass that makes up most of the piece represents the idea that what is visible is not even what is important. One might imagine that the legs of the woman (assuming there is a woman) are propped on a car door and she is seeing a reflection of Ron Cey and Ken McMullen through her rear-view mirror. The two third basemen of the then National League champs are obviously in good spirits. But in the right corner of the "mirror," one barely sees the tip of the cap of Jerry Royster, the* third *third baseman of the team, a rookie, fighting for a job.*

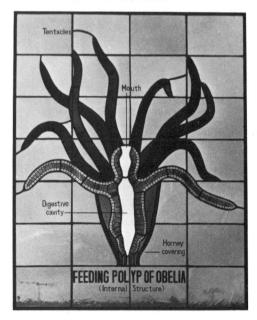

9

Peter Mollica

Peter Mollica installing a leaded panel in a Berkeley, California, residence.

Peter Mollica is a central figure among West Coast glass artists. It was one of Peter's windows, in fact, that planted the idea-seed in my mind that something new and different *is* happening in stained glass. Most of the innovative glass artists are just now breaking into their aesthetic territories, whereas Peter has been producing mature, unique work since the late 1960s.

Peter considers himself primarily an architectural glass designer. He worked as an apprentice to the Chris Rufo Studio in Boston from 1964 to 1968. Most of his training was done in Gothic Revival styles for churches, as the popularity of stained glass in private environments was not widespread at that time. To round out his formal training, Peter traveled to Germany to observe closely the contemporary approaches of the master German architectural glass designers. Mollica has successfully blended his educational experience with traditional glass into a style that fits naturally the informal manner of West Coast living.

Though his preference may be the architectural window, his prolific working pace has produced numerous autonomous panels, and, most recently, he has moved beyond the single dimension of the leaded window by designing and constructing a free-standing stained-glass garden sculpture.

"Friendly formality" might be the descriptive phrase for Peter's aesthetics. The "reserve" of formal design mixes with the unpretentiousness in Peter's personality to produce the unique spirit of his glass compositions. There is also an ease to his design mannerisms; his windows fit everywhere, from public buildings and private homes to the rear window of his Volkswagen bus (wherein you can find a Mollica family portrait in stained glass).

I design my windows as an integral part of architecture, and in residences, as part of the daily lives of the people who live there. I want my windows to be beautiful. The designs seek to employ the qualities of the glass so that they contribute to the total effect of the environment, to the overall intent of the building, the room, and the lives of which they are a part.

I'm involved with two different design methods now: an analytical, rational method that I feel works very well for public buildings, and a more personal, intuitive method I've used for years when designing for residences.

The analytical method is very important to me now because I am interested in doing larger windows for public buildings. Windows in public buildings require design that responds directly to the forms and intent of the architecture.

As most of my work, up to 1976, has been for residences, I have developed a less formal, more intuitive method of designing which considers not only the architecture but also responds directly to the personalities of the people who will live with the window.

10

I have lately discovered that the two methods are not incompatible, and I think they will soon become one.

Living room window.

This window faces south and receives direct sunlight most of the day. The room is white and has many windows facing San Francisco Bay to the west. It was necessary that the stained glass help to control the strong sunlight from the south. The use of grays and blues helped to reduce the glare and heat of the sun and to keep the room cool on hot days. The leaded glass is framed and mounted against the existing plate glass window, which provides additional insulation.

Stairs.

As you enter the house through the main entry, you see the lower right hand portion of this window. As you walk toward the stairs, the forms of the window lead you up. As you arrive on the landing in front of the window, the strong diagonal form describes or "assists" your motion as you turn to continue up to the second floor landing. As you descend, the process works in reverse.

While responding to forms of the architecture, (the diagonal of the staircase, etc.) the design speaks as well about the everyday activity that the window oversees and reinforces. I hope it makes the usually automatic act of going upstairs or down a little more enjoyable and a little less automatic.

I like to do windows that are not focal points of a living room to be stared at while lounging, but rather situated so that their viewers come upon them, perhaps a little unexpectedly, with different frames of mind. It seems to me that no matter how they are feeling, coming on this window will change them a little. They will constantly see new and, I hope, exciting things about this window as it becomes an important part of their lives. The strong yellows and whites in this north-facing window help to brighten up the stairway. The opak (semi-opaque) glass helps conceal the neighbors' house directly across from the window as well as adding interest to the exterior facade, as seen from the sidewalk of this very pleasant residential street.

Stairs. 1975. Berkeley, California, residence.

Living room window. 1971. Berkeley, California, residence.

Tub window. 1975. Oakland,
California, residence.

Garden sculpture. 1976. Palo Alto, California, residence.

Berkeley Glass. 1974. Pebble Beach, California,
residence.

Tub Window.

The tub is a deep Japanese-style bath in which you submerge your whole body in very hot water. The window was designed with cool colors as a relief from the heat of the water. I felt that strong hot colors would have been too confining and oppressive. The blues and variegated whites allow the mind to wander in meditation or delight. The steam rising from the water fogs the glass and gives it a misty quality which fits well with the whole experience.

Berkeley Glass.

This panel combines various "white" glasses; opak, opal, seedy, reamy, etc., as well as a machine-rolled pattern glass which I call BERKELEY GLASS because I got it from the Berkeley Glass Company, whose shop is near my studio.

The pattern is of many small convex squares that seemed to fit well with the leaded-square forms I used across the center of the design. This panel was not made specifically for the house. It is one of many panels I make without commission. It is mounted in a dark redwood frame and is meant to be hung in front of a window. It is easily moved, or, as we say in California, recycled to some other location.

12

Dan Fenton

Dan's stained-glass career began by accident. He had been trained as a photographer but was out of work and desperate when he was offered the unlikely job of assembling glass bathroom fixtures for tract houses. He accepted the job and soon found himself fascinated with the glass scraps that were thrown away. From an assemblage of discarded commercial glass Dan constructed his first window, without the aid of classes, instruction books, or tutor.

Walking into Dan's studio is like experiencing a chapter of a Jack Kerouac novel. The studio and living space are a single cluttered environment situated atop a furniture factory in one of Oakland's seedier commercial districts. To meet with Dan, to get to know him, I adapted to his nocturnal working hours. I would arrive late at night and experience the overstimulating effect of the atmosphere that surrounds Dan and his work. Along with the mixed collection of windows, tropical plants, work tables and benches, beer and wine, Goodwill furniture and assorted junk, there are invariably people "hanging out" in his studio. These characters, ranging from law students to life's dropouts, listen to his jazz records or watch him work. A crazy, energized scene, but Dan seems to thrive on it, producing an art that is dependent on daylight in the middle of the night.

Dan is renowned among his stained-glass peers for being an extremely fast glazier and a talented fisherman. His fascination with the ocean and deep-sea fishing has been the inspiration for many window designs. For example, *Spirit Dance* is the result of a vision he had while watching the surf at Big Sur. In his enthusiastic manner he described to me his next major window project: a surrealistic bird's-eye view of a school of ling cod swimming over New York City.

I want my windows to change character as the light changes. Although I am using imagery that is possibly more suited to oil on canvas, painting lacks that characteristic of change. In no other medium can one use the light as effectively as with glass.

Getting stained-glass shows is difficult because nobody knows how to deal with it. Art critics don't know what to say about it, show jurors don't know what to think of it, and installation directors don't know how to display it.

THE PASSING OF MIGRATORY SOUNDS

This window is sound imagery inspired by music. I was really into Miles Davis's music then. Imagine musical sounds taking on a visual shape. This one is a composition of form in space analogous to the way music is made up of sounds moving in a matrix of time.

The Passing of Migratory Sounds. Collection of the artist.

Dan Fenton

13

Spirit Dance. Collection of the artist.

Charting of the Subterranean Movements of Heavy Metal. Collection of the artist.

Dan Fenton preparing to sketch his next subway-map window.

DRUID OAK TREE

This was commissioned by a poet who had a strong fascination for the Druids. The Druid people were really attuned to the workings of the earth—the seasons, the sun/moon cycles; and they were tree worshippers, the oak tree being their favorite. This composition was designed not for a space but for a particular person. That's something that is often overlooked in commissioned art.

CHARTING OF THE SUBTERRANEAN MOVEMENTS OF HEAVY METAL

When I was in New York City, the subway guide was a vital part of my urban survival kit. Contrary to the prevailing opinion of the locals, I really got off on riding those dirty and noisy trains. Maybe it was the thunderous rumbling of steel against steel, or maybe seeing those bright blue flashes of electric discharge that happen on rainy days.

The composition was inspired by the straight-line style used by many stained-glass designers in the East. I thought maybe I could come up with a composition that would be a "tipping-of-the-hat" gesture to those designers. I saw the subway guide as a masterpiece of graphic design, so I enlarged a section of the midtown Manhattan map and translated it into stained glass.

Now I'm working on a subway map of my own design. It will be of the same nature as the first subterranean landscape, but it will contain routes that go in circles, lead to dead-ends, and follow collision courses. It is to be a design for rapid transit that is guaranteed to be totally impractical and unfeasible. I plan to present it to the city of Los Angeles in a proposal for a rapid-transit system.

Druid Oak Tree. Cupertino, California, residence.

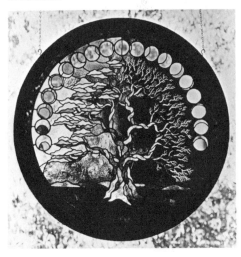

15

Casey Lewis

Casey considers his first sixty windows "glazing exercises" or his own self-conducted apprenticeship to the glass medium. His introduction to stained glass began with a how-to-do-it book, which led to tutoring from glass artist Peter Mollica and eventually the invaluable tour of German windows to which most architectural glass designers treat themselves.

Casey's architectural windows have evolved steadily toward a technique no other glass artist uses. Casey is the first to use the enameled (colored) lead line as an integrated compositional element of his finished window panels. Since the craft's inception stained glass has been treated as a medium of transmitted light and color only. More recently, some architectural designers have used reflected light and the lead line as design factors . . . but none have used the lead line as part of the textural and reflected *color* composition. This breakthrough in technique is exciting in itself, but Casey's compositions of color, line, and form are, in the final analysis, architectural statements: windows that draw from the unique elements of a building as their main purpose for being.

Aptos residence.

The elements within my compositions are an extension of the architecture in which they are set. The delicate and tentative intersections of wall upon foundation and of roof upon wall are the architectural subject matter of the Aptos windows. The sheet copper that rims the amber transparent glass and the amber opaque glass replaced the black glass I had intended to use. I wanted a third element to result from the tension generated by the balance of the forms. Black seemed a negative embodiment of balance, and the reflectiveness and color of the copper helped to unify the windows.

Exterior view of windows and entryway. 1975. Aptos, California, residence.

Sauna panel. 1974. Lafayette, California, residence.

Dennis Hartelius

Doorlite. 1975. Lafayette, California, residence.

Front door. 1976. Concord, California, residence.

Casey Lewis and partner Ellen Flagg in their Lafayette, California, studio.

Bedroom window. 1975. Oakland, California, residence.

Sauna panel.

   The window separates a sauna from a hallway lit by a skylight. The opal-flash glass is translucent, and the gray light that reflects off the surface in the hall is very different from the bright blues seen from inside the sauna. The circular window shape gave me a chance to bring the rectilinear structure of a wall into a circular space while simultaneously implying the extension of the circle into the wall. To only extend the wall through the circle would be to ignore the circle's very real presence. The linch-pin of the composition is the cluster of white arc forms. They exist in the space that echoes the circular shape of the opening, but they are ordered by their reaction to the forms that are an extension of the wall.

Doorlite.

   In designing the Lafayette window I sought to juxtapose the clarity and austerity of the white-painted interior and gray-brown stucco exterior with the natural-ness of the amber objects within the home. The diagonal roofline provided the vehicle for the contrast.

Front door.

   The home commissions I have done over the past five years have made me aware that the concept of the lead line as a silhouette against the glass may be true in a church where the leaded glass is the only source of light, but it is not true in most domestic architecture. Artificial light and light from adjacent windows cause light to reflect off the surface of the lead of most leaded glass in homes. Identical lead lines are painted red and blue on both sides of the Concord window. From either side, as the less flamboyant reflected light replaces transmitted light, the painted lines state the basic composition.

17

Dennis Hartelius

Sanford Barnett

It has been fascinating to discover that many of the new glass artists have been unaware that others are, like themselves, challenging and testing the conventional boundaries of traditional stained glass. Most often this is simply the result of the accidental physical distances between artists. Sanford Barnett is one artist who has chosen to live and create his art far from his peers.

Sanford makes his stained glass in a small agricultural town nestled in California's coastal foothills, about two hours' drive south of San Francisco. His studio is an old dairy barn in the backyard of his century-old Victorian farmhouse (complete with a white picket fence). I suspected that in this turn-of-the-century environment only turn-of-the-century windows would be the aesthetic rule. But Sanford is defining his own artistic territory, working with as much sophistication as any "city" artist.

Sanford is primarily self-taught in the techniques of stained glass, having made a natural transition from the hard-edge paintings he produced in college to glass and lead. He had produced mainly architectural commissions, but recently he has favored exploring the autonomous window panel.

Sanford has taken stained-glass iconography to its furthest limits by using the glass itself as the central subject in his compositions. The full, uncut sheet of hand-blown glass has its own inherent beauty. Sanford, not wanting to destroy the indigenous aesthetic of the glass sheet, has produced a series of windows that are simply assemblages of uncut glass sheets leaded together.

1975. Pacific Palisades, California, residence.

I am attempting to use the more or less traditional techniques of stained glass in very untraditional ways. I am now working with the medium directly and spontaneously, often eliminating entirely the protracted method of reproducing a painted or sketched design in stained glass. I have begun to incorporate whole sheets of glass, broken sheets, and pieces of scrap, as I find them, unmanipulated. I make liberal use of the controlled accident, where the materials determine the creative process as much as the hand and the eye. Also, I have abandoned the all too prevalent notion that stained glass must be beautiful. This has freed me to explore. For example, I can accept and work with the humor generated by the simple juxtaposition of a formal, austere sheet of German opak glass with the suggestive and grotesque qualities of an odd-shaped sheet of a poured, domestic glass. The hair-like leading then grows out of the relationship of the glass with itself, as an organic, self-generating process.

I no longer necessarily see my panels as "windows," but rather as "things in themselves." I am experimenting with artificial light and non-transparent glass and see this as a legitimate solution to the problem of separating the medium from the

Sanford Barnett stretching a lead came strip in his studio.

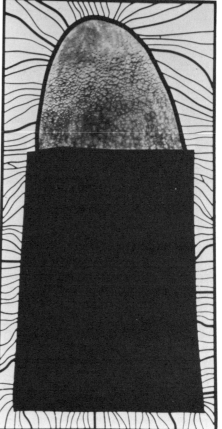

Thornprikker's Nose. 1976. Collection of the artist.

confines of architecture. Given the state of American architecture, it is the autonomous, non-architectural approach to stained glass that offers the most productive orientation. This movement away from architecture is positive, but difficult, for it requires a redefinition of what stained glass is. Like painting or sculpture, stained glass should be seen as a medium of artistic expression that needs no contextual (architectural) justification.

19

Narcissus Quagliata

Narcissus was twenty years old, a painter, and anxious for change when he immigrated from Rome to San Francisco in 1962. Since then he has earned his master's degree in fine arts from the San Francisco Art Institute, has hand-built a home on the northern California coast, and has shifted his creative focus from painting to stained glass.

Narcissus now makes his home and studio in an artists' community in an industrial section of San Francisco. Dominating his expansive studio are windows in every stage of development, from conceptualizing sketch to finished and mounted panels. Sketches of future windows and completed drawings shingle the walls; layouts and patterns of full-scale windows along with both full and shattered sheets of glass carpet his floor. The scene is like a demonstration of how to make a stained-glass window from idea to finished product. Narcissus reverently observes every stage of a window's evolution, savoring the effects and the visual quality and feel of the processes.

The finished windows, the products of Narcissus's applied processes, differ from his contemporaries' windows in two major ways. First, his autonomous works are unusually large, sometimes two or three times the dimensions of windows made by others.

Second, there are no other new glass designers using the human figure as the central iconography of their subject matter.

Most generalities are deceiving, but Narcissus is the physical embodiment of the much romanticized archetypical artist. He is bizarre in habit and casual in appearance, has a European accent, and is at least slightly narcissistic in his self-image. Meeting with this artist-image was entertaining. Narcissus sat in his throne-like chair (which swivels and has a structurally unsound back) while I faced him across a small, junk-encrusted table, balancing myself on a stool. Smoking his French cigarettes, he indulged me by sharing his dream-images, his ideas, and critical perspectives.

Working with glass pushes me closer to myself and other people. I work in glass because I love both the material itself and the light that goes through it. I love the way glass breaks, cuts, shatters; I love its transparency and opacity.

I enjoy working with glass because it gives me the chance to speak to the viewer at his or her core, directly. Light is a universally understood language; it takes no special education to respond to it —just being alive. To me a great deal of the value of the medium lies in its capacity to produce a profound and primal pleasure.

Glass wants to crack a certain way, so let it crack that way. . . . Everybody wants to repair windows when they break, but why? At the most just put lead lines

Narcissus and his son standing in front of the unfinished *Stained Glass Suicide*.

where the breaks are, as they have done in the restoration of cracked medieval windows. I love those spider web cracks that crawl up and down the glass windows of the Middle Ages, interrupting the consciously-designed compositions. The way those windows were originally was beautiful, but now with all those leaded cracks running through them they are even more so.

There is "mind" in its pure form creating order and harmony, then there is material in time—cracking, moving, stressing, and creating its own commentary on what the work is all about. So, if you are aware of this relationship between mind, material, and time, not only can you consciously enjoy it, but you can utilize it as an important tool in approaching your work.

In every stage I'm making judgments and being sensitive to the material, so that the process of working does not separate conception and execution; rather, my work is constantly being conceived and is constantly being executed. For some reason we have the idea that art is disconnected from the flow of things, when in reality it's always plugged in. I like keeping this in mind as I flow from material to material in the different stages of making a window. To me, even the cartoon must be beautiful, as well as the pattern pieces and the unleaded window easeled against the light.

Ideas and images come from others to you, from your mind to the paper, and then to the glass. In the process of glazing, the whole image changes quality and feeling. You finally install the finished product. It looks good or not, it could crack or not, it gets photographed, then this total image is reproduced, say, on a piece of paper like the one you're looking at in this book. Somebody views it and may or may not be affected by it, but it does not look anything like the original window and even less like the idea that was behind the creation of the window. But the process goes on and this image travels, metamorphosing through people's minds, through glass, through paper, through photographs, etc., and then finally the energy abandons it. The window in time will disintegrate; its reproductions will end up in dusty attics or second-hand bookstores and nobody will care anymore, and that will be that. . . .

I enjoy working on commissions as well as on my own independent panels, because I don't feel really human unless I partake of two different kinds of activities— one, being with other people and in situations that are challenging and unfamiliar to me; and the other, being completely alone and exploring that with my work.

Commissioned work is always exciting because I can sense the usefulness and pleasure that my work can bring to a living space, private or public. And the audience is already there! But it puts me under some strain because it constantly tests my capacity to relate to others. I must be able to make a relevant contribution to their environment that in a way comes from them and yet is expressed through me.

Too much commissioned work drives me crazy. It's like a life without any privacy at all, without hidden moments that are so special, without dreams at night. In my studio, alone with my own work, I feel free to experiment—to fail and play while exploring the subtle, sensuous, and sometimes disquieting areas of my own self. It feels good to be free, even at the risk of having no audience. My independent panels come out of this abandon.

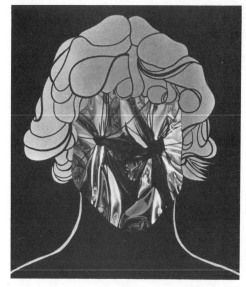

Ink and silver-foiled drawing of the future window, *Neil: A Study for a Portrait in Glass.*

Eva. 1975. 4 × 6 feet.

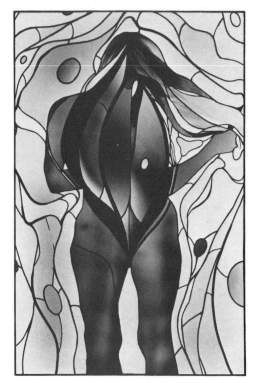

21

I enjoy working with the human figure and have been surprised that such a small number of stained-glass artists have really worked with it in depth. The figure is a subject you can't miss on. Everybody's interested simply by being interested in themselves. But I don't like to impose on the glass a figure or any image without allowing the glass still to be itself, material as material, with a nature of its own. Or just light as light.

My Androgynous Shadow, which is actually my shadow, comes from my feeling of being half-man, half-woman, with an outer character that is masculine and an inner self that is feminine. The window grew out of this intense meshing of the different parts of myself, which became clearer to me through two dreams I had.

> *Floating on the surface of the sea, facing the blue daylight sky, a cut begins forming on my body, lengthwise. A vagina opens me up, parts me in two, and it keeps opening until I can see the night sky through it and below me. As if sucked by the vacuum, the sea water begins rushing through me, falling toward the stars below, dissipating in the void.*

> *Walking along the Tiber in the old quarter of Rome, a sandstorm catches me, and in the fierce wind the old city fades away. Now I am alone on a ledge. I watch my black shadow stand up and walk away from me, I turn into a woman, and decisively, without looking, leap backwards into the void.*

Full view of *Dancing, Dancing, Dancing . . . San Francisco Cabaret 1972-75.*

My design Dancing, Dancing, Dancing . . . San Francisco Cabaret 1972-75 is an homage to a magnificent night club and dance hall that used to be in San Francisco's North Beach. I am just presently committing this design to glass, and with it I hope to convey the love I have for the San Francisco night life, especially as it was at "Cabaret," unreal, tacky, filled with unceasing free-form choreography, feeling in its purest form, finally rid of content! (Let it go! Let it go!)

There in a dim multicolored light you could be anything —man, woman, androgynoid, animal; choose your own role from your shadow self. For a few hours you could take on any identity and live it out. You merged in the sea of bodies, moving and dancing, in the glitter and the light and the incessant beat of the music. The atmosphere was truly a stupendous narcotic and I am sure the luminosity of glass is perfect to express that unreal atmospheric glow, and the brittleness and fragility of glass is a perfect parallel to a reality so unstable and volatile, cracking and peeling away.

To me, my work is a way of going further and further back to the source, where everything is alive, possible, present, and never predictable.

22

JAD KING   Untitled Victorian panel. Reworked 1975. 26½ × 43 inches.

JAD KING   Interior view of *Tree Mandala*. 1973. 6-foot diameter.

JAD KING   Exterior view of *Tree Mandala* and domes.

JAD KING
Solvang, California, residence.
View of entryway and living room.

JAD KING   Solvang residence.
1975. The round center panel
is 5 feet in diameter.

PAUL MARIONI *Homage to Chicken Little*. This window is located in Paul's kitchen. It you look closely, you will see that the sky is cracked glass.

PAUL MARIONI *Dali*. 1971.
Collection of the artist.

PAUL MARIONI Detail of *Dali*.

PAUL MARIONI *Sink*. Private collection, San Francisco. The plumbing is actually a formed plastic tube that contains water (near the top of the tube you can see the water line).

28

PAUL MARIONI *25 Years.* Private
collection, San Francisco. This
panel was commissioned for a 25th
anniversary gift from
husband to wife.

PAUL MARIONI *25 Years.* Detail.

29

PAUL MARIONI *200 Years*. 1976.
Collection of the artist. This is
the first of its kind. It is the result of
Paul's recent attempts to eliminate
the lead line from his work
altogether. The experiments were
conducted at the A.C. Fischer
glass factory in Bramche, Germany,
in February 1976. Paul developed
this process with the help of master
glass blower Werner Gewohn
and his assistant, Hans Gewohn.
The experiment was made
possible by a grant from the
National Endowment for the Arts.

KERRY KELLY *Clouds.* Victoria, British Columbia, residence. This tiny window is tucked into an unlikely corner of a pantry.

KERRY KELLY Detail of *Clouds.*

FRED ABRAMS *The Nervous System of a Chambered Nautilus.* Collection of the artist.

LOWER
EXPECTATIONS
PLANETARY
REALISM
O.B. Rigan

FRED ABRAMS Untitled. Collection of the artist.

PETER MOLLICA   Living room window. 1971. Berkeley, California, residence.

PETER MOLLICA   Stairs. 1975. Berkeley, California, residence.

PETER MOLLICA *Fiberworks*. Installed in a garage door, these windows mark the entryway of a private school of basketry and weaving, Berkeley, California.

PETER MOLLICA   Tub window.
1975. Oakland, California,
residence.

PETER MOLLICA   Dining room window. 1976. Berkeley, California, residence.

PETER MOLLICA   An architect's office at home. 1973. Berkeley, California, residence.

DAN FENTON *Charting of the Subterranean Movements of Heavy Metal.* Collection of the artist. Here the window hangs in a bagel shop in Berkeley, California.

DAN FENTON   *Seashell Patterns*. Dining room, Los Angeles residence.

DAN FENTON   Entryway. 1975.
Fresno, California, residence.

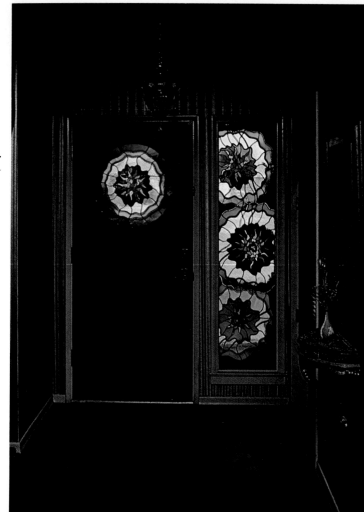

DAN FENTON   Entryway. Detail.

41

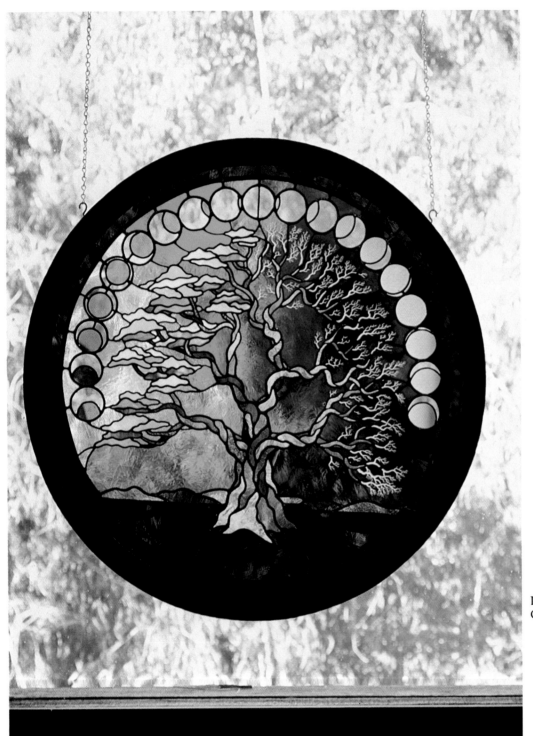

DAN FENTON *Druid Oak Tree.*
Cupertino, California, residence.

CASEY LEWIS   Sauna panel. 1974. Lafayette, California, residence.

Dennis Hartelius

CASEY LEWIS   Aptos window. Detail.

CASEY LEWIS   Front door.
Exterior view showing enamel-
painted lead lines. 1976. Concord,
California, residence.

CASEY LEWIS   Front door. Interior
view.

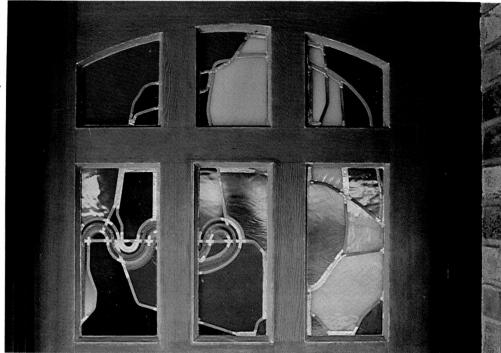

SANFORD BARNETT   Entry hall window. 1975. Pacific Palisades, California, residence.

SANFORD BARNETT Untitled
autonomous panels. 1976. Collection
of the artist.

SANFORD BARNETT Exterior view
of Pacific Palisades residence.

Jean Meyers

Narcissus Quagliata The artist next to the incomplete panel, *Androgynous Shadow.*

Narcissus Quagliata
Androgynous Shadow. Detail.

NARCISSUS QUAGLIATA   A corner of the artist's glass studio, San Francisco.

Narcissus Quagliata   Stained-glass environment. 1975. San Francisco residence.

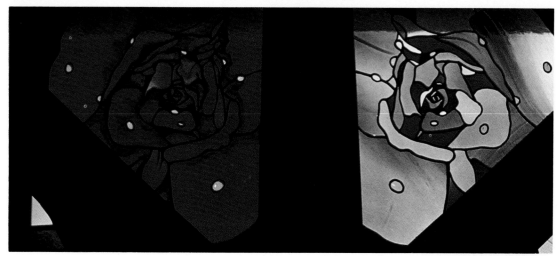

Narcissus Quagliata   Stained-glass environment. Detail.

Narcissus Quagliata   Sitting room
adjacent to stained-glass environment.

Narcissus Quagliata   Stained-glass environment. Detail.

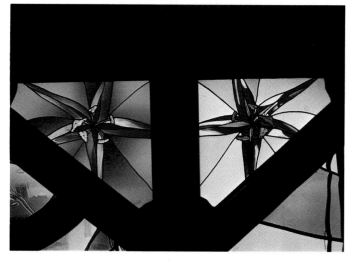

MARK ADAMS Baptistry window.
All Saints Episcopal Church,
Carmel, California.

MARK ADAMS   Stairwell window. San Francisco residence.

JUDY JANSEN Entry hall windows,
18 × 18 feet. 1976. San Marino,
California, residence.

JUDY JANSEN Detail of entry hall windows.

54

KRISTIN NEWTON   *Calligraphy-Beyond Words.* 1976. Collection of the artist.

ROBERT KEHLMANN *Composition X.*
Private collection, New York City.

Robert Kehlmann

ROBERT KEHLMANN   The artist
with a work in progress.

56

ROBERT KEHLMANN *Composition XXII.* Collection of the artist.

ROBERT KEHLMANN *Composition XXI.* Collection of the artist.

Robert Kehlmann *Composition XXVIII*. Collection of the artist.

TERRY MARKARIAN Study. Point
Richmond, California, residence.

TERRY MARKARIAN Living room.
Point Richmond residence.

TERRY MARKARIAN Untitled autonomous panel. Berkeley, California, residence.

O.B. Rigan

TERRY MARKARIAN Detail of autonomous panel showing hand-blown rondelle and beveled crystal.

O.B. Rigan

60

ELIZABETH DEVEREAUX TALLANT   Untitled autonomous panel. 1975. Private collection, San Francisco.

ELIZABETH DEVEREAUX TALLANT *Argonne Window.* 1974. Long Beach, California, residence.

ELIZABETH DEVEREAUX TALLANT *Argonne Window.* Exterior view at night.

ELIZABETH DEVEREAUX TALLANT   Living room window. 1972. Collection of the artist.

RICHARD POSNER *The Meyer Library Window.* 1976. Collection of the artist.

RICHARD POSNER Detail, *The Meyer Library Window.*

RICHARD POSNER Detail, *The Meyer Library Window.*

RICHARD POSNER *The Treadwell Hall Window.* 1976. Collection of the artist.

Ed Carpenter   Main entry hall window. 1975. Portland, Oregon, residence.

ED CARPENTER   View of window from backyard garden. Portland residence.

ED CARPENTER   Interior view of entry doors. Portland residence.

ED CARPENTER Untitled
autonomous panel. 1976. Private
collection, Portland, Oregon.

ED CARPENTER   Experimental autonomous round panels. 1976. All are 30 inches
in diameter. Collection of the artist.

ED CARPENTER   Dining room bay window. Portland, Oregon, residence.

ED CARPENTER   Entryway windows. 1974. Mono County Courthouse, Bridgeport, California.

Ed Carpenter

PETER WICKMAN *Sidewalk Cascades*.
1972. Collection of the artist.

PETER WICKMAN The artist
with an autonomous panel in
which he utilized polarized
two-way mirror glass (the inverted
triangular shape) and his slumped
glass process. 1976.

KATHIE STACKPOLE BUNNELL
Envisioning a Marriage. 1975.
Collection of the artist.

KATHIE STACKPOLE BUNNELL
Envisioning a Marriage. Detail.

72

KATHIE STACKPOLE BUNNELL *Childhood Icon*. 1975. Collection of the artist.

KATHIE STACKPOLE BUNNELL
Childhood Icon during its easeled
stage.

73

KATHIE STACKPOLE BUNNELL
Tears. 1975. Collection of the artist.

KATHIE STACKPOLE BUNNELL
Chain of Events. 1974. Collection of
the artist.

KATHIE STACKPOLE BUNNELL
Buckeye Tree. 1974. Zen Center,
Muir Beach, California.

OTTO B. RIGAN Six of 20 window openings. 1976. Olzack Bros. Liquor and Deli, Atwater, California. These windows are the result of a collaborative effort by architect Rod LaSalle, Cummings Studios, and the artist. The windows are traditionally crafted but use recently developed glasses.

OTTO B. RIGAN Wine room windows. 1976. Olzack Bros. Liquor and Deli.

<small>BILL CUMMINGS   Front door. 1968. San Francisco residence.</small>

BILL CUMMINGS   Exterior view
of door at dusk.

Judy Raffael   Untitled
autonomous panel. 1975. Private
collection, San Geronimo,
California.

Judy Raffael   Chapel doors.
Detail.

JUDY RAFFAEL   The Salvation Army Chapel doors, San Francisco.

DICK WEISS   The artist with broken and rebuilt versions of the same autonomous panel.

DICK WEISS   Untitled autonomous window panels. Collection of the artist.

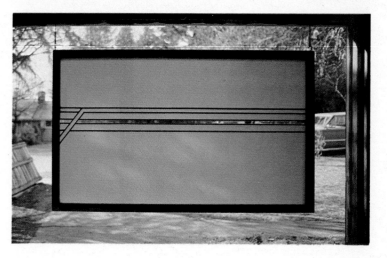

81

James Hubbell Doors. 1974.
Triton Restaurant, San Diego.

James Hubbell Exterior view of Triton doors.

82

JAMES HUBBELL Skylight. 1974.
This art dominates the main dining
area of the Triton Restaurant.
The building was originally a bank,
later a photo-supply store. Jim's
challenge was to reshape the
building to reflect the mood of the
sea, to create an interior that
resembled the underside of an
ocean wave. On the final day of
construction, he surprised the
work crew by arriving with both
arms loaded with crystal beads that
were strung together. Like a
baker frosting a cake, he finished
the interior by draping these
prism-casting beads under the
skylight, over the entryway doors,
and throughout the bar and lounge.

JAMES HUBBELL   Dining room window. 1972. Greenery Restaurant, San Diego.

JAMES HUBBELL   Entry doors. Greenery Restaurant.

JAMES HUBBELL   Outside view of entry doors, Greenery Restaurant.

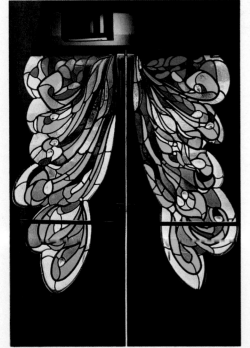

JAMES HUBBELL Shower skylight
and wall (partial view). 1976.
Hubbell residence.

JAMES HUBBELL Stained-glass-and-concrete sunscreen. Hubbell residence.

JAMES HUBBELL Entry to boy's bedroom, door closed. Hubbell residence.

JAMES HUBBELL Entry to boy's bedroom, door open, Hubbell residence.

Mark Adams

Mark Adams' range includes the mediums of tapestry, stained glass, and painting, from the monumental to the intimate in scale. He is a well-known and respected artist in the San Francisco Bay Area and has achieved international recognition for his tapestry designs.

A native of Fort Plain, New York, Mark studied under the painter Hans Hoffman and the revolutionary French tapestry artist, Jean Lurcat. In 1946, Mark hitchhiked to California and worked as a ditchdigger and elevator operator to support his artistic ventures. He has had one-man exhibits in many of America's most venerated museums and galleries. He lives and works in a restored nineteenth-century firehouse in San Francisco with Beth, his artist wife.

Mark's work seems a true manifestation of himself. His personal demeanor and his windows both contain an intense reserve, an authority. Yet, even the monumentally scaled works reflect a humaneness, an openness that is as informal and warm as the West Coast's climate.

Mark is not represented here by a personal statement. He preferred not to let his philosophical perspectives get in the way of the visual statements he has already made.

Beth Adams

Mark Adams in his studio with a tapestry design.

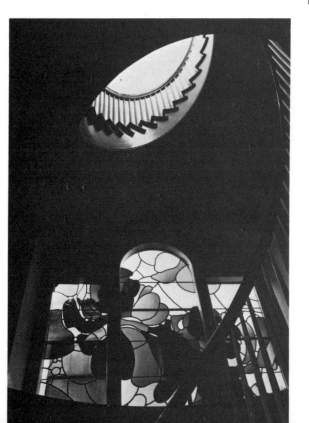

Stairwell window. San Francisco residence.

West window. 1973-74. Temple Emanu-el, San Francisco, California. One of two major windows that face each other across the Temple. This window was designed around the theme of "fire." The east window's theme is "water."

Judy Jansen

The challenge of incorporating dimensional blown glass into the leaded-glass panel has been met with taste and skill in the architectural panels of Judy Jansen. Judy, who trained as a sculptor and later as a glassblower, is the only artist I know who combines these techniques in a single panel without creating a gaudy overstatement. Her windows are beautifully juxtaposed compositions of sculpted, sensuous shapes within a field of slightly tinted flat glass.

Judy creates the mouth-blown shapes at a friend's studio, but most of her work is done in an adapted one-car garage behind her brother's home in Whittier, California. Every square foot of her studio is well organized and functional. When I visited her, she was constructing an eighteen-foot-square window for a residence in Los Angeles—a monumental work in a mini-studio.

It seems natural to me that stained glass progresses more into the third dimension. We already have two dimensions, length and width, and maybe even the fourth dimension, a time-space atmospheric quality that glass seems to have. Except for a little lead surface relief and faceted glass, the third dimension of depth has not been fully explored.

The complexities of glass account for its fascination as well as its counter-attraction. Glass in certain states, like broken, splintered, or shattered, can seem somewhat hostile. Communicating that glass is friendly and inviting, not only in the first, second, and fourth dimensions but also in the third, is exciting to me.

Stained glass is a delight for the eye, and for the touch as well. The more senses one can add to interpreting and appreciating stained glass, the closer we are to total communication.

Judy Jansen soldering a blown-glass shape into a window panel.

Detail showing relief of blown-glass.

Autonomous panel. 1974.

Kristin Newton

Kristin Newton with her louvered room divider. The divider is eight feet high and eight feet wide, and is motorized so that each vertical louver is in constant motion. Its name is *Calligraphy-Beyond Words*.

Different phase of *Calligraphy-Beyond Words*.

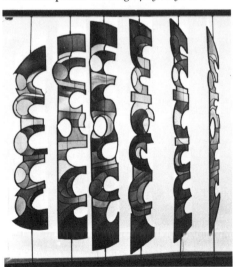

Kristin works a self-regimented eight-hour day at her commercial glass studio in North Hollywood, California (a few blocks from Universal Studios). During working hours she sells supplies to hobbyists and helps manufacture commissioned "commercial" or "production" windows. But that is only part of her day. When the shop closes, she religiously turns to her own exploratory glass projects and begins the role that is her real interest, that of the artist-designer-craftsperson, without critical or commercial restriction.

Scattered about the studio are a number of pieces that are the result of her nocturnal efforts. Most are three-dimensional, multi-layered windows that are as much sculpture as stained-glass art. Her favorite projects to date are a series of stained-glass louvered windows. In redesigning the conventional louvered window with colored glass and odd shapes, Kristin has merged aesthetic challenge with practicality: her window becomes a changeable, kinetic composition as it is opened and closed to ventilate a room.

I think the most important thing is keeping one's integrity as an artist. That is why I prefer autonomous windows. For me, they are the only true way to growth. There are no rules but the rules you create for yourself. You don't have to compromise. You only have to pose questions and find answers.

I love movement, the kinetic effect of overlapping colors. Geometric window shapes bore me. I find free-form shapes and negative spaces far more challenging.

I have always related to glass in abstractions. It would be interesting to deal with recognizable images, but I just seem to think in the abstract. With the non-objective, color and form stand alone. Also, I think I am not open enough to let my emotions be made public. With realistic images, my emotions might become obvious. With the non-objective, I can deal with whatever I'm feeling through color and design. These emotions may possibly be subtly relayed to the viewer, but not in a dramatic soul-baring way.

The fabrication process is as important as the design process to me. Very often, spontaneity and creativity happen between the glass and me. I can never relate to a window if I have to let someone else do the fabricating. It hasn't come out of their soul. It's just a job to them.

If a window is truly mine, I have to see it through the whole process, even the cementing. After it's finished, there is such an anticlimactic feeling. It usually takes at least a month before I can even think about the window again. I become totally separated from it, it's a thing of the past. The creation is definitely the most important part of it for me. I may enjoy a window very much after I've made it, but it's never the same.

90

Robert Kehlmann

Robert was a writer before becoming involved with stained glass. After receiving his M.A. in English literature (from the University of California at Berkeley), he treated himself and his wife to a vacation in Europe. It was from this trip that Robert's interest in stained glass evolved.

Robert's aesthetic sources are intricately related to contemporary painting, but his introduction to the medium of stained glass was in a short how-to-do-it course for the beginner. After a year-and-a-half of experimenting and developing techniques he decided the medium could be approached in the tradition of the serious studio painter. He then rebuilt the interior of his small garage, installed a pot-bellied stove and some work tables, and began producing his unique interpretations of stained glass and its potentials.

Robert's panels are not "windows" in the sense that you can see through them. You cannot—but you cannot avoid making eye contact with

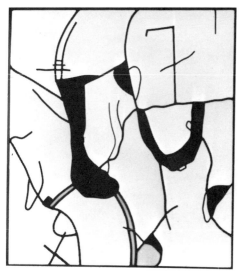

Composition XXVI. 1974. Collection of the artist.

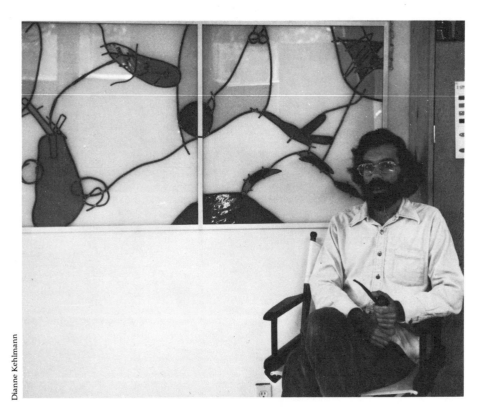

Dianne Kehlmann

Composition XXXIII. 1976. Robert Kehlmann and leaded panel commemorating his birthday.

91

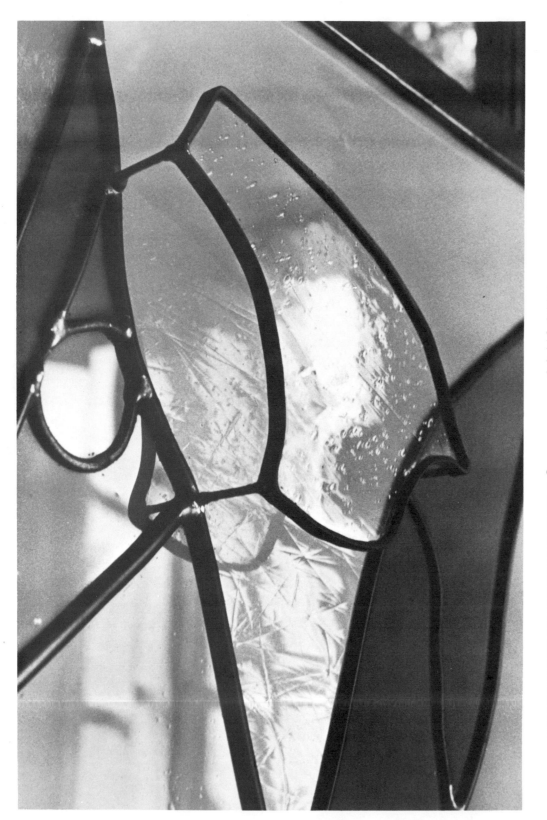

Detail of elevated glass shape.
Most of Robert's work has a layered
dimension. Small shapes of glass are place[d]
one to two inches from the surface of the
leaded panel, creating a surface dimensio[n]
and new colors and shapes as the glass piec[es]
overlap and influence one another.

Composition XXVIII. 1976. Collection of th[e]
artist.

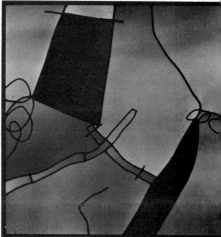

them either. He does not design his autonomous panels as decorative objects that play secondary roles in an environment. Instead, they are mounted and viewed, throughout his home, like paintings in a gallery; panels to be viewed and considered for their serious intentions, not their beauty.

Often an academic, which Robert is, will attempt to capture the spirit of naiveté. Some of Robert's panels do have that feeling of simplicity. This element in his compositions is a result of his pedagogic approach to problem solving and the exchange of drawings and ideas with his twelve-year-old son. Robert's son makes crayon drawings and gives them to his father as gifts. Robert uses parts of these as the starting point in many of his sophisticated panels.

Composition XII. 1975. Collection of the artist.

My windows are architectural only to the degree that a painting or a piece of sculpture placed inside a building is architectural. There is no reason why stained glass should have any limitations beyond those dictated by materials and a sensitivity to design. The traditional approach to stained glass as a secondary art, "the handmaid of architecture," has forced many designers to feel the need to restrict or architecturally justify their work—even when making autonomous panels. It has impeded a healthy and creative exploration of the medium. Only recently have such explorations begun. Painting on glass, for example, has yet to be examined. Chagall makes paintings on glass. He doesn't design with glass.

Painting depends on reflected light. Traditionally, glass has relied wholly on transmitted light. Certain painters—and they are of great interest to the glass artist—have explored transmitted light. Van Gogh looked at the sun and painted it. Rothko's canvasses quiver from the light emanating from them. Rouault's Christs sometimes glow. Reflected light, in turn, is of interest to the glass artist.

The German flashed "opak" (translucent) glass that I use permits my windows to have a different effect with transmitted light than with reflected light. I design with both types of lighting in mind, selecting my glass for its translucent and reflective qualities. The personalities of these works alter throughout the day in response to the changing quality of light.

I don't use transparent glass because I don't want people looking through my windows. What lies behind the compositions, aside from a source of light, has no relevance to my design.

My elevated forms and lines permit me to explore a wide range of visual concerns that are difficult to broach given the physical restrictions of glass and lead. Through relief I can activate underlying forms, mix colors and textures, redefine both negatively and positively the shapes of underlying pieces of glass, or pull the eye across a heavy line, permitting two differently colored pieces of glass to read as a single form.

Traditionally, the leading of stained glass has been concealed around form. Now designers like myself are drawing with lead. My lead lines do more than merely hold pieces of glass together.

93

Terry Markarian

Terry Markarian in his Point Richmond, California, studio-home.

Soon after graduating from high school, Terry began working evenings as an apprentice to master craftsman Sal Sigstedt, who counseled Terry to work hard, preferably in his own home, and to refrain from copying other artists. Terry respected his mentor's advice. In the nine years since his apprenticeship ended, he has worked long hours in the basement studio of his wood-shingled home, making architectural and autonomous windows in relative isolation from other glass artists.

This isolation has nurtured a unique technique. Terry became fascinated with the time-consuming process of beveling crystal glass, a process so intricate that the craft has been all but abandoned since the early twentieth century. Terry combines beveled glass (which he makes himself) with mouth-blown rondelles (disc-shaped pieces of glass that are hand crafted by Terry's friend Donald Carlson) and German-made antique glasses. He is the only artist I have found who uses these three materials, in non-traditional ways, as part of an integrated palette.

It is impossible for words truly to reflect what I think my work is about. I've just returned from a trip to Europe and my ideas have been turned around 360 degrees. We saw all the standards—Chartres Cathedral, Notre Dame, the German windows. . . . But how can I say it? At 37,000 feet I saw the northern lights from the 747 window. I was glued to the window for hours. That is what excited me, that is what I want to do, a window that is always moving, changing like the aurora borealis. Now I'm frustrated by the realization that I could never do the northern lights.

Half Moon Bay, California, residence.

Elizabeth Devereaux Tallant

Elizabeth's glass studio is a small room in the farthest corner of the house she shares with her husband and children. Her stained-glass windows are everywhere: the living room, bedroom, over the kitchen sink, and, of course, in the studio. In this earthy home that is full of the character of the family that lives within it, Elizabeth's windows are simply part of the organic whole. A comfortable home with comfortable windows.

Elizabeth has often said that, to her, glass has a suggestive, sensual quality. She feels a natural affinity for the medium. She selects her glass intuitively and carefully. The glass often determines the window she designs. This is the quality in Elizabeth's windows that draws me to them. They are not of a single style, nor are they a product of an intellectualized process. Her windows are a sensitive response to the innate, subtle qualities of glass.

Elizabeth's oval-shaped autonomous panel is a commentary on the woman in herself, a visual investigation into her own varied characteristics.

Early in 1976, Elizabeth and her family were caught in the center of the catastrophic Guatemalan earthquake. From this experience she now plans an "earthquake series" to mark her increased respect for Nature.

My work varies quite a bit from window to window. Often I have commissions for a particular environment where I must be conscious of the mood of the room and the colors in it, as well as of what's going on outside the window. I also try to be aware of the people I'm designing for. Often they are people I know. This allows me to put some of them into the window as well as myself. Other windows are "glass paintings" in a sense that they are not for a particular environment, but are purely personal expressions of art in glass.

Stained glass allows me a kind of artistic freedom that painting never did. I find it easier to face the "drawing board" than the canvas, since I usually have a client with specified limitations of size, shape, setting, and color, and often a preference as to theme. All of these things provide a structure within which I begin to work. Rather than confining my designs, these limitations provide a secure structure for me to work out of. It probably is similar to a child being raised with a strongly defined set of rules or expectations as opposed to one with a very undefined set. At least, the former has something to rebel against, to test, or to confirm.

Living room window.

When we moved into our house, the picture window in our living room looked past our side yard straight into our neighbor's picture window. I wanted privacy without cutting out the light or the view of the trees above or the garden below. I had

1975. Private collection, San Francisco. If you look closely, you will see that the window is actually two separate panels divided by a diagonal, lightning-like shape. This diagonal shape is a space with no glass in it.

worked with mirrors before, and felt mirrors in the middle were the ideal way to block out their view of us. (Besides, I have always liked the idea of confusing viewers at first, making them look more closely and discover slowly what is happening.) Then I left the top and bottom very light gray or clear to allow the maximum light in, as well as to again play with the viewers' perception. I wanted them to see three planes at once: mirror—totally reflective; translucent or blurred—creating a flat plane level with the window's surface; and clear—throwing the eye outside, beyond the room. I realized that in essence I was dealing with sculpture since the inside and the outside were an essential part of the design, making it a three-dimensional illusion.

The color as well as the design were influenced by Japanese art, and especially some wonderful Japanese pottery I once saw.

Bedroom window.

I designed this window the first year I started stained glass, but executed it four years later. For me, this window has a playful feeling. I have always been inspired by Paul Klee, and I think you can see some of his influence in the window, though it was unconscious when I designed it. I have also come to the conclusion that when I am drawn to an artist's work, it is essentially by what he or she reflects of my own vision.

Other influences in the window could be my love for discovering colored mushrooms under beds of damp leaves or finding an exotic Rousseau plant under which a ten-legged redbird beetle is hiding.

ARGONNE WINDOW.

I did this window for a building my brother designed. His work has been inspired in part by Adolph Loos, a Viennese architect and designer around the turn of the century, who also inspired those who went on to start the Bauhaus movement. I had Loos's style in mind when I began designing the window as well as my brother's request for ''something a bit more static in line, more dignified in feeling than some of

Living room window. 1972. Collection of the artist.
This window changes character completely from day to night. At night the stained glass assumes the darkness of the outdoors, the mirror glass reflects the light in the room, and the lead lines become more apparent than in daylight.

Bedroom window. 1973. Collection of the artist.

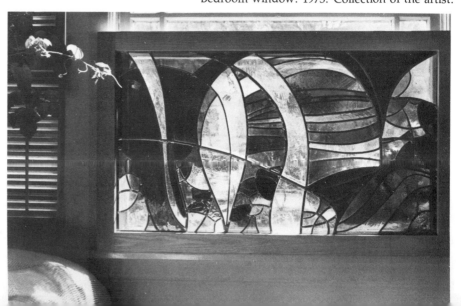

Argonne Window. 1974. Long Beach residence.

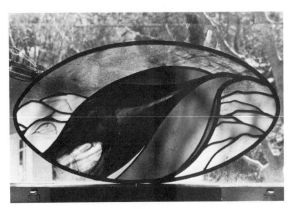

1975. Private collection. San Francisco.

*your other work." I began designing from left to right. As I got to the middle a curve
with more motion and emotion surfaced. I repeated, more or less, the design again on the
right, but with even more motion, like a "variation on a theme." The design is very
suggestive of music to me, as well as of the feeling I got from Loos's work.*

*Again, I wanted to work with very subtle value changes in gray, white,
clear, and mirror. Much of the motion is created by the glass textures and the mirror.
From the outside at night the mirror looks black. I tried to combine the mirror shapes
with the lead lines to make a strong and changing linear effect.*

*At night, from the inside, I also wanted the window to have a "life of its
own," different from the day. The white opaque glass becomes gray, the mirror, light
and reflective, and totally changing with the environment, while the clears and grays
move with the light reflecting their strong textures. I like this window a lot because
it seems strong and pure to me.*

1975. *Private collection. San Francisco.*

*I have a strong emotional response to this window. To me, it is an expres-
sion of the woman in me. I see it as very female and sensual in the forms.*

*Sometimes, I will go glass buying and treat myself to a special piece or two
of glass that I react strongly to. In that case, it is the glass that will suggest my design,
and I must bend to its life. I really loved the two pieces I bought for this window and
though I had to change the surrounding glass a number of times, I was scrupulously
careful to have it come out as I envisioned it. One of the sheets covered a range from
very light flesh tones to a deep orange with a thin vein-blue layer. I cut pieces of this
for each side. In the middle of the window is the other piece, which was mostly deep
tissue—like reds and browns, with this beautiful light shape blown into it.*

*The forms are suggestive, yet they seem to suggest different images to dif-
ferent people.*

*In German, there is an expression, "That was a difficult birth." This
window exasperated me in the process, but once it was done, it was very hard for me
to part with it, almost as if it were one of my own children.*

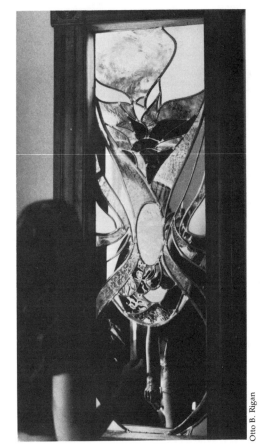

1975. San Anselmo, California, residence.

97

Richard Posner

Richard has been working with blown glass for six years and with stained glass for a little over one year. He is currently working in a not-so-private area in the glass-blowing studio on the campus of the California College of Arts and Crafts in Oakland.

The process of making a window is many stages, requiring great amounts of time and skill. These factors are magnified by the complexity of the window's design, the number of pieces per square foot, or the use of intricate or odd-shaped pieces of glass. Most glass artists agree that the process itself is a laborious necessity leading to the pleasures of experiencing a finished window, but Richard not only respects but also enjoys the process, imparting his unique visions to all stages of window making. Eventually, he says, he would like to design a window that mirrors the process itself: a window that utilizes the smell of the flux, the pattern paper, the tools he uses.

Richard's windows show a respect for technique and offer fascinating subject content, but they are also designed to go specific places. But the windows are not extensions of the walls, nor are they truly autonomous. They are, as Richard explains them, "picture windows," stained-glass vignettes reflecting the artist's documentation and interpretation of what he sees and feels, placed in the real world.

I grew up in the Los Angeles of the 1950s. Visiting there recently recalled many sights and sounds: hours spent flying kites made out of the old LOS ANGELES MIRROR newspaper; making boats from Dad's scrap-pile and launching them at Westlake Park; hearing the songs of the meat man, the fish peddler, and Jolly Jack, the ice cream man with a rubber dagger in his back; and climbing Watts Towers with an older brother who was (and still is) an artist.

I see my work as a diary of my relationship to my environment, internal as well as external. My sources lie in the cultural polarities between the refined vocabulary of art and history, and the popular vocabulary of ongoing activities such as newspapers, chance conversations, and reflections in windows. The finished pieces represent my effort to transform and reinterpret these languages, and in so doing to probe the nature of experience. I want to explore the glass canvas both as a window and as a portrait.

Durston Saylor

Richard Posner in his studio at California College of Arts and Crafts.

Lana Feldon

His Master's Voice. 1975. Collection of the artist.
Edgar Allan Poe, when asked what the most beautiful word in the English language was, replied "cellar door." Posner juxtaposes Poe's imagery with Nipper, the curious dog, to create an anthropomorphic self-portrait of the artist waiting for Godot.

Il Papa Nomina Trente Cardinali. 1975.
Collection of the artist.
A headline torn from the San Francisco Chronicle was united by Posner into a marriage combining his love of baseball and Italian culture.

The Big Enchilada. 1976. Collection of the artist.
This work is a thinly-veiled allegory about Watergate, done in the tradition of northern Renaissance art, wherein each image is pregnant with symbolic meaning. *The Big Enchilada* (Mitchell) is being fought over by two German shepherds (Haldeman and Ehrlichman), while Magruder holds the ethical-moral compass and a shadow lurks at the taped door of the Democratic headquarters.

Durston Saylor

The Meyer Library Window. 1976. Collection of the artist.
Here Posner looks back on an injury suffered while doing alternative service as a conscientious objector.

Ed Carpenter

This artist's studio can be found in a refurbished, old white church on the outskirts of Portland, Oregon. He and a close friend (an excellent woodworker) bought the building and converted the loft, congregation area, basement, and adjoining parsonage into individual work spaces. "The Cream of Mushroom Church," as it is called by locals, is currently shared by a consortium of artists, craftspeople, and architects.

Ed's stained-glass windows are architectural art. He takes this approach seriously, studying the language of the architect with as much energy and interest as his inquiries into the medium of lead, glass, and color. As part of his self-conducted apprenticeship, Ed was twice a pilgrim to Europe, where he visited glass factories, window installations, and stained-glass artists. In 1975, he worked under the private tutelage of Ludwig Schaffrath, Germany's leading glass designer.

Subtle, yet powerful, Ed's mature and confident architectural panels seem to grow from or belong to the environments in which they are set. His windows are accurate yet personal responses to the character of a building and its effect on people. They show his mastery of the material and his ability to understate strength.

Portland residence

Here's a situation where the glass plays an interesting role in the relationship between an entry and a garden, both designed by Richard W. Painter. He conceived the project in terms of layers that progressively reveal the interior or garden while maintaining a certain visual suspense. To achieve this he developed the idea of leaded-glass entrance doors aligned with a leaded window on the opposite wall of the vestibule. A visitor approaching the house is given views through and around the doors that only suggest the nature of the interior. Once inside, a glimpse of the garden is possible through the more transparent parts of the window, but the garden's full extent is not revealed until one reaches the main part of the house. You might say the glass serves as a negligee, the approach being as interesting as the arrival.

Having formulated this basic plan, Dick called me to discuss the glass design and such related matters as night lighting and the effects of the planting when mature. In one of these talks we hit upon the subject of combining stained glass with reflective bodies of water, and within a few days Dick had designed a pool to be placed outside the south-facing window and to nest against an existing capped well. The pool would not only help complete the sitting area on the garden side, but would also cast reflections of sunlight from its surface through the colored glass. By pushing the window out one foot from the wall Dick was also able to break up this long shingled surface and further integrate the progressive elements of the entry: doors, vestibule, window, pool.

Architectural glass artist Ed Carpenter in his studio.

100

My own first concerns were to design the placement of the mullions and to find ways of integrating the basic skeleton of the glass design with the architecture. I liked the form of the pool around the well and decided to develop it by making my composition essentially a stack of these nesting circular forms intersected by horizontals that would extend into the window the movement of the wall. In placing the circular forms on the right and the horizontals on the left, I was trying first to help "turn" people

1975. Portland, Oregon, residence.
This photograph shows the relationship of the entryway windows to the glass-walled hallway that links the garage and the main section of the home.

Exterior view of entry doors.

Entry doors opened, revealing second window panel.

View of window from the backyard garden.

through the graphics of the window to the left and down the hall in the direction of the house; and second to compose forms that would work from the opposite side as well, both as part of the outside wall and as reflections in the pool.

Dick had pointed out to me that an entrance is frequently a good place for an increase in scale for the sake of definition. My design for the doors was therefore an attempt to make this jump in scale while maintaining a strong relationship between doors and window. We had agreed previously that the doors should be made of transparent glass in order to respect the general transparency of the front entry wall, and to give a filtered view of the window behind.

This job was unusual for me in that the architect—in this case landscape designer—took the glass seriously from the outset as an integral element of his design. He consulted me early enough so that the glass was not simply crammed in at the last moment to block some unwanted view, and we developed a relationship during the job that allowed for some growth of the original ideas. Of course, we were immensely helped throughout this process by an eager and accepting client.

Chapel windows. 1974. Christ Episcopal Church, Lake Oswego, Oregon.

Karlis Grants

Autonomous round panel. 1976. 30-inch diameter. Collection of the artist.

102

Peter Wickman

Peter, when he began to work with glass, wanted to learn the fundamentals of a craft that no single studio or school could provide. His studies took him from his native Denver, Colorado, to Ohio (where he studied math and physics at Antioch College), New York City, Philadelphia, Great Britain, and Sweden. A superb craftsman, he now has a studio in an industrial warehouse near San Francisco's Embarcadero.

Most of the window designs Peter created and constructed during his well-traveled apprenticeship were traditional, from Art Nouveau panels and Neo-Gothic church windows to a "window hanging" of Paul Bunyan's baby blue ox. I don't think Peter was ever comfortable with these conventional approaches to window making. This structured, historical orientation exhausted his creative patience. When he made his break from the traditional his impulse was to exercise his freedom by summarizing all his pent-up creative ideas at once. His first truly original panel was a flood of ideas blended together. He calls this turnabout window (*Sidewalk Cascades*) his "expression of frustrations."

My latest works are experiments in exploring the natural phenomena of light. My ideas come from nature—not from the graceful rhythmic patterning found in field and forest but from the fundamental awareness that nature is supreme. No matter how determined we are to create our own static but dependable environment, the forces of nature will return it to its proper place. Decay is an aspect of life against which we continue to struggle. In this struggle there is formed a spontaneous random pattern of shape, line, and texture, the best examples of which are found on sidewalks, streets and walls. It is this random, spontaneous movement that gives form to my images.

The content comes from the foundations of the mind, illustrated in children's drawings done before the age of seven. During these early years, children in all cultures are more subjective in their interpretation of their environment. And all over the world they use very similar images in their drawings. I see these images as fundamental archetypes of the human race.

The random structuring, decay, and restructuring of our artificial environment, coupled with these elemental images of nature, are the foundations for my images.

Peter Wickman explaining his method of slumping glass. The clay form he is holding is the desired shape to which he wishes a piece of glass to conform. The flat glass is placed over the clay shape, then set into a firing kiln where it is heated to the melting point of the glass. The red-hot glass becomes flexible and drapes itself over the clay form, assuming its relief shape. Peter utilizes slumped glass in most of his window panels.

Sidewalk Cascades. 1972. Collection of the artist.

Detail of an unfinished panel that selectively utilizes slumped glass for an interesting low relief.

Kathie Stackpole Bunnell

Kathie is the sophisticated, mature version of the flower child, the contemporary embodiment of that which was good in the late 1960s. She is as friendly and open as her art.

Her home and studio reinforce this image. Nestled into a wooded hollow at the base of Mount Tamalpais in Mill Valley, California, Kathie's home is a Hobbit's fantasy, a rambling, hand-built log and rock structure with shingled turrets and steep peaks for a roofline. A circular, rough-hewn wooden stairway leads to her second floor stained-glass studio. In this small studio Kathie creates the most intimate windows I have ever seen.

Her meticulousness and skill are mythic to glass artists who know her work. With her window *Envisioning a Marriage,* for example, she spent a patient five hundred hours in construction. After cutting the glass (some 954 pieces!), she felt that part of the glass used for the netting was the wrong tint. Realizing a change was necessary, she cut a replacement color, an accomplishment of incredible patience out of a desire for aesthetic perfection.

For me, Kathie's work in glass is a diary of her intimate emotional responses to the life process—a visual realization of what *she* is about.

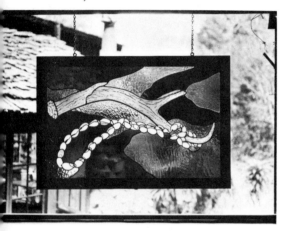

Chain of Events. 1974. Collection of the artist.

I want my stained-glass windows to keep implying, unfolding, and changing. They should be revealing themselves through time, not stopped dead in solidity. They should be like the super-cooled liquid that is glass itself.

I want my windows to have motion in them. Things being in a state of motion, in a state of living and dying at the same time, interest me. The way I see it there is a kind of network structure that living substance articulates and makes alive, and that is left behind when the living substance dies. It's like a cactus plant that dies and leaves behind a kind of skeletal woody structure that's full of holes you can see through.

Energy forms in nature interest me—the geometry of crystals, the sedimentary designs of mud put down in layers through time, vortices, and waves. I see these as dynamic processes wherein materials go through alternating periods of infusion with activity and relative rest. The transformation of matter through stages of life corresponds with the development that goes on in each of us.

The destruction and breakdown of things interests me. I think every artist is involved with that. When you're making a creative thing, there's also a destructive element in the very fact that things are being changed. It's like the process of being born, breaking out of one world and into another.

As an artist, a person has the chance to change his or her life by acts of will. Through the glass work I can realize a commitment to life in a certain way. My work is a reflection of problems I have and things I love.

Kathie Stackpole Bunnell.

104

Buckeye Tree. 1974. Installed at the Zen Center, Muir Beach, California.

Childhood Icon. 1975. Collection of the artist.

Original crayon drawing of *Childhood Icon*. 1948. Collection of the artist.

CHAIN OF EVENTS

I often like to use three elements in design. CHAIN OF EVENTS includes a shell necklace, an antler, and a wave pattern. Each of these elements is a separate thing, but they fit together. The wave element is time motion. I feel movement to be the most constant thing there is. The antler is weathering and returning to earth. The shell necklace is a kind of infinity symbol. It doesn't stop, but keeps winding around the antler. It's continuous and has no break in it.

BUCKEYE TREE

The window was inspired by a tree I planted outside my house. It went for a season or two without my paying much attention to it. Then one winter we had a warm spell that brought out the buds at the ends of the branches. Going outside in the warmth and seeing the buckeye with its very bright green leaves made me give up work on one window, start this one, and get caught up in spring.

In the winter, because I spend more time indoors, I tend to do things that are in heavier colors and not quite so airy. They tend to deal with abstractions and the synthesis of inner goings-on. Then I'll get tired of that and want to do the opposite. While I worked on the buckeye, which is made of very light tints of reamy glass, I kept envisioning the same window in black light, ultraviolet colors. This was the opposite wanting to have its say too.

CHILDHOOD ICON

The crayon drawing already looked something like a stained-glass window. It was at my parents' house; a four by six-inch drawing that I did in 1948 at age seven. One day I was thinking about how philosophical children are and what wonderful

Envisioning a Marriage. 1975. Collection of the artist.

105

Passion Flower. 1973. Private collection, Oakland, California.

Detail showing the miniature scale of the *Passion Flower* window.

Tears. 1975. Collection of the artist. Outside view of the window installed in Kathie's living room.

thoughts they come up with. I thought of this drawing and how it now expressed to me a highly ideal sense of human potential: a crowned, winged being enthroned on a wheel or sun and surrounded by strong colors.

The crayon drawing is daring in the use of a wide range of unlikely, mysterious colors, yet balanced. It has dynamic motion and symmetry set askew and returning to itself. After all, we are made that way ourselves —bilateral symmetry set in motion and never quite symmetrical because we are constantly changing and growing.

Envisioning a Marriage

Envisioning a Marriage is describing a commitment to form a union between inner and outer, all the opposites, black and white. It started with a network as a positive thing, akin to the nervous system in which we are caught and yet through which we perceive everything. ("Through" is one of my favorite words!) The hand touched the net, changing its shape. As the hand, through an act of will, perceives the net, the result becomes creative energy, represented by the garden (a meditative landscape seen on the back of the hand). I made this window to clarify the use of free will for myself. Will, here, is respectful and appreciative of life's patterns (the network). Marriage refers to a ceremony within oneself and a dedication to the creative forces in the garden.

The original idea was to explore networks that are breaking or fraying or being pushed through. It's something like metamorphosis, like caterpillar-chrysalis-butterfly. The chrysalis opens and the creature that was once inside leaves behind its shell, the empty transparent substance.

Tears

Tears is based on a haiku about seeing the Milky Way through a tear in a paper window. It is based on a grid pattern and resembles a Japanese shoji screen, but within it are places where the grid pulls apart, revealing glimpses of night sky with stars. These openings are birth spaces for the mind or gateways for new feelings.

Bill Cummings/Hilda Sachs

Bill and Hilda depart from the other glass artists documented here in two major ways: first, they are trying to maintain in a large studio an atmosphere conducive to the creation of artful stained glass; and second, they work *together* as interdependent artists/designers. Bill's image of the ultimate stained-glass studio is a place for spontaneous work on a very large scale—the production of works that a single artist, acting independently, could not achieve.

Cummings Studios was founded by Bill's father. It is located in an unlikely corrugated metal warehouse, in the light industry district of San Rafael, California. The feeling of the studio, from the inside looking out, contrasts sharply with the used-car lots, body-and-fender repair shops, and boat marina that dominate the area. The studio consciously works at creating a relaxing and workable atmosphere. Often I've walked through the industrial-like entryway to discover an environment filled with sounds of classical piano being performed live specially for the working craftspeople.

Hilda, who was raised and educated in Berlin, has worked as a stage designer (Berlin), a fashion designer (London), and a designer of wallpapers and textiles (San Francisco). She served a formal apprenticeship with Cummings Studios starting in 1952 and has been working with stained glass since that time. Bill was educated as a musician. After finishing college in 1964 he studied with his father for four months until his father's sudden death. Bill and Hilda have been working as a team since 1968.

We have known each other since 1952. Our close working relationship began in the midst of individual and collective emotional turmoil and struggle. As we work together it is increasingly evident that the idea of community works. Individually we can only grow as fast as we allow or push ourselves. Together we spark ideas in one another and the growth is staggering—this is truly an example of 1 + 1 = 3. As our working relationship has grown, so has our studio situation, and working together with five other people we are able to demonstrate wholeness and totality as we never would have imagined.

The rules we play by demand a coming together with no preconceptions in approaching new problems. They demand total loyalty, dedication, openness and trust—to ourselves, to one another, and to our individual and collective aesthetic aims. In our community we are in a continual state of equilibrium/disequilibrium. We find we are continually strangers and continually changing, but is this not the basis of a good piece of art? Stained glass is our way of life—through this medium we are expressing our lives, our aims, our hopes.

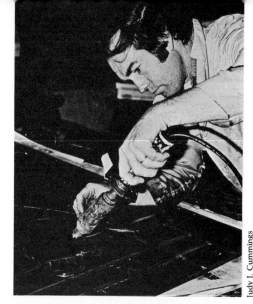

Bill Cummings glazing a leaded-glass panel.

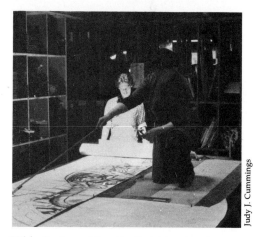

Hilda Sachs putting the finishing touches on a full-scaled window design.

Kitchen window. 1974. San Anselmo, California, residence. Designed by Hilda Sachs and built by Cummings Studios.

107

Judy Raffael

Judy, her husband Joseph (a painter), and their children live in a brightly colored home dwarfed by a grove of redwoods. A stained-glass panel hangs over the porch among multicolored banners, suggesting a pageant and presumably celebrating life. The studio, a short walk from the house, is large and light and is divided into equal parts for both artists. Judy is a painter, a quilter, and a stained-glass artist.

She began her glass involvement by serving a traditional apprenticeship. Soon after, she found herself designing large commissioned works. She felt that much of herself went unrealized while designing such large windows, so recently she has limited her stained glass to small, more intimately-scaled panels.

Judy is excited about the results of her experiments with the stained-glass medium. These experiments deal mostly with her desire to omit the lead line from the stained-glass panel. Her excitement has been contagious, spawning the stained-glass careers of her friends Paul Marioni and Kathie Bunnell.

The most important thing for an artist is to evolve in the most personal way possible, so that what you're doing is peeling off the layers of yourself to get to the nugget that lies within. To work on a large scale is exciting but you have to work with so many people—architects, committees, a strict budget. The result is always diluted. The artistic impulse is stopped short.

I realized that the best thing to do would be to get away from everybody, close myself in my studio, and open to myself to find just who I was. It's terrifying but it's necessary for every artist to do this for at least some period of time.

Birth Window.

A friend, a woman I have known for years, had made a film of the birth of a baby (the mother giving birth was also a close friend). She showed me the film on a projector that can freeze the movement if you want and she would arbitrarily stop it at certain points. I thought it would be interesting to use a "freeze" from the film and make a glass window out of it. So I made two windows, each slightly different, for the filmmaker and the woman who had the baby.

My window border designs are a frame for the image. I'd always been interested in medieval glass borders. They do something wonderful to the interior of the piece. Most of the time they create a lot of light-energy around the central image of a window. Many contemporary windows have a feeling of bleeding off their own edges. But these have a border around them that contains them, commanding your eye to zero in like a bull's eye to the target.

Birth Window. 1975. Private collection, San Geronimo, California.

Untitled. 1975. Collection of the artist. The photo-image is a portrait of Judy's daughter.

108

Dick Weiss

Dick makes his autonomous panels in his garage whenever he has time off from his job as a railroad switchman. He has been making windows for four years. Even with the rigorous physical demands of his job, he manages to produce a panel every two weeks. Between the railroad, his glass work, and his family there remains little time or energy for marketing his windows. He has sold only four windows in as many years. The remaining eighty-odd windows are stored in his garage/studio. That doesn't seem to upset Dick, a self-taught artist who feels that the four years of work has been his apprenticeship. Every stage of his development seems more exciting to him than the last and a prelude to the next.

June and Dick Weiss in the artist's studio.

My main obsession has been to produce something beautiful in glass.
I have thus far experienced a three-stage development (sounds like a rocket, doesn't it?). I first started making mostly design-oriented, Art Deco windows. Then I decided to push myself a little, and a period of experimentation followed. During this stage I painted on windows, glued on glass and other objects (such as T-shirts), and in general tried to loosen up. Then, finally, I entered the third stage, which I am still

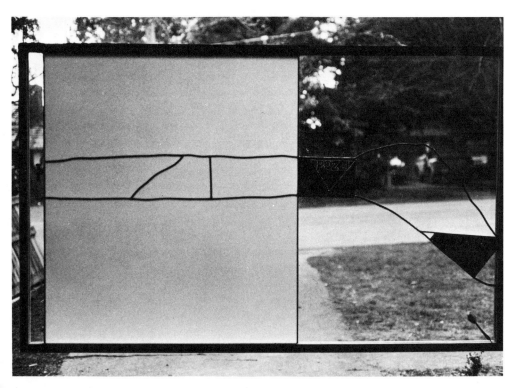

Pozzi. Collection of the artist.
Dick was dissatisfied with this panel, unsure of what it needed for a finishing touch. His brother, also pondering the problem, struck a dart into the lower-right corner. That satisfied Dick.

Untitled. Collection of the artist.

Untitled panel from Dick's loosening-up
stage. Collection of the artist.
Yes, that's a T-shirt.

in. I call this stage my abstract-expressionist-minimalist stage. These are lots of words,
but then minimalism has always been characterized by word overkill.

My best windows have been influenced by the polarities of Francis Picabia
and Mark Rothko. Picabia was a Dada star, but his work extends far beyond Dada. He
refused to take style clichés too seriously, poking fun at studied mannerisms of art.
But there was plain beauty in his visual touch. He was good. On the other end of the art
spectrum, on the take-art-as-seriously-as-religion end, there is Mark Rothko. Beautiful
colors, beautiful forms, the power of the ego. He was good, too.

I like to keep things simple. Simple and geometric. "Less is more," as Mies
van der Rohe said. . . although occasionally I feel pangs of fear that maybe "less is a
bore," as Robert Venturi quips. I weary of geometrics sometimes. But still my windows
have progressively become more simplified—my last one only had two pieces of glass in
it. It might be ground zero. I don't know. I'll go somewhere else from here, probably
toward the energy of color. When the critics write about Mark Rothko's paintings, they
invariably mention how "alive" his paintings feel, as if there were a light emanating
from the painted forms. Well, in stained glass the light does come through your forms.
No "as if"—it literally "lights up" your forms. The colors can be astonishing.

I seem to like simple forms. Even if I try to be messy, it is always a simple
mess. That's just the way I am. Whatever I do, I'm sure I'll keep it simple. Simple and
powerful and, perhaps at its very best, meaningful.

110

James Hubbell

James Hubbell defies exact definition. He designs stained-glass windows and buildings; he is a poet, a painter, a sculptor, and a visionary thinker. He conceives, then constructs, usually by himself, total environments in which his stained glass is only a supportive part, an instrument used to complete a whole. The "whole" is a testament to his personal visions and dreams, an attempt to mesh the rational, function-oriented world with the aesthetic perspectives of his artistry. Few details in his environments escape his touch. He carves and shapes walls, mosaics the floors, designs the sink basins, the doorknobs, the fountains, the furniture—all the elements that will contribute to the finished effect. Jim is the master of an organic contemporary-baroque style.

His aesthetic has had a postive effect on an incredible number of San Diegans. As we researched and photographed his stained glass and environments, we were barraged by willing observers with tales of Jim's prodigious contributions to every kind of environment imaginable, from restaurants and

Finished panels in Hubbell's glass studio.

111

dentists' offices to banks and sorority houses. Jim has said he would even design a bus stop—anything to further integrate art and life.

Jim hitchhiked through Europe and Africa when he was barely out of high school, in the late 1940s. It was that first trip abroad that introduced him to the architecture of Antoni Gaudí in Spain and the windows of Notre Dame in Paris, both major sources of inspiration for his environmental designs. He served fourteen months in the Korean War, most of that time painting monumental murals "all over the place." He never did a stained-glass apprenticeship nor did he finish his formal school in art. In the mid-fifties Jim and his musician wife moved onto ten mountainous, undeveloped acres fifty miles inland from San Diego. Since that time he has created a half-dozen fantasy-like buildings for himself and his family on their land.

It is difficult to discuss stained-glass windows with Jim without including his philosophical perspectives on humanity, habitat, and art. To best describe his feelings about his work we finally selected the following poem, which was written and printed by Jim as part of his booklet *Love Letters to the Earth,* a selection of his poetry that he shares with his friends.

James Hubbell.

I give you My friend
My heart
to hold with distant hand.

For you
Your life must be a gate,
Your work an open door.

Upon it I will carve
All Heaven   a firmament.
Upon it will crawl the snail.
Will break   the wave.
Upon it will pass
The hand of man   The dream of God.

If my heart were the door
to all of life,
enter it.

I would   if I could
Give it all to you.

112

Stained-glass and concrete sunscreen shading a picnic area that adjoins the Hubbell family swimming pool. This living, working, and playing environment was built entirely by the artist.

James Hubbell's studio and storage area. The right half of the adobe and ferrocement structure is the sculpture work area and the left half is the stained-glass studio. The small conical-shaped building to the left of the studio is a "storage closet" for everything from small experiments in glass to scale models of visionary buildings.

This swirling, weathered brick wall is part of the exterior of the Greenery Restaurant. Although the mediums of brick and glass are very different, the windows of the restaurant and this wall pattern have a similar visual feel.

Stained-glass and shingle pillar. Greenery Restaurant, San Diego.

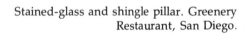

114

All Souls Episcopal Church. Point Loma, California.

115

A NOTE ON THE PHOTOGRAPHS

I had been photographing stained glass for about seven years when I was approached with the possibility of doing this book, so I could anticipate the problems involved.

I learned to avoid using diffusing screens behind the glass. What is gained by reducing the difference in densities between various pieces in the window does not make up for the loss of beautiful texture in the fine hand-blown glass.

Each window posed different problems: waiting for the right light, trees too close outside, eaves casting shadows, horizon lines, clear or light yellow glass next to a deep blue or red, and the need to balance the interior light with daylight.

I used Kodachrome 64, reflectors, stands, cords, umbrellas, floods, flash, obscenities, and finally I had to do what I learned at the knee of my guru, Bob O'Shaughnessy, which Otto made the battle cry of this book: spray and pray.

Charles Frizzell

Portrait of Frizzell by Peter Mollica

Graphic Credits

This book was electronically composed by Chapman's Phototypesetting, Fullerton, California. The text type is VIP Palatino, a computer adaptation of a face originally designed for hot-metal composition by Hermann Zapf. The full-color process separations were supplied by Northwest Color, Menasha, Wisconsin. The book was printed and bound by George Banta Company, Inc., Menasha, Wisconsin. Production was supervised by David Charlsen. The design is by Anita Walker Scott.